YUEN WOO PING'S
Wing Chun

Hong Kong University Press thanks Xu Bing for writing the Press's name in his Square Word Calligraphy for the covers of its books. For further information see p. iv.

THE NEW HONG KONG CINEMA SERIES

The New Hong Kong Cinema came into existence under very special circumstances, during a period of social and political crisis resulting in a change of cultural paradigms. Such critical moments have produced the cinematic achievements of the early Soviet cinema, neorealism, the *nouvelle vague*, and the German cinema of the 1970s and, we can now say, the New Hong Kong Cinema. If this cinema grew increasingly intriguing in the 1980s, after the announcement of Hong Kong's return to China, it is largely because it had to confront a new cultural and political space that was both complex and hard to define, where the problems of colonialism were uncannily overlaid with those of globalism. Such uncanniness could not be caught through straight documentary or conventional history writing: it was left to the cinema to define it.

Has the creative period of the New Hong Kong Cinema now come to an end? However we answer the question, there is a need to evaluate the achievements of Hong Kong cinema. This series distinguishes itself from the other books on the subject by focusing in-depth on individual Hong Kong films, which together make the New Hong Kong Cinema.

Series General Editors
Ackbar Abbas, Wimal Dissanayake, Mette Hjort, Gina Marchetti, Stephen Teo

Series Advisors
Chris Berry, Nick Browne, Ann Hui, Leo Lee, Li Cheuk-to, Patricia Mellencamp, Meaghan Morris, Paul Willemen, Peter Wollen, Wu Hung

Other titles in the series
Andrew Lau and Alan Mak's *Infernal Affairs – The Trilogy* by Gina Marchetti

Fruit Chan's *Durian Durian* by Wendy Gan

John Woo's *A Better Tomorrow* by Karen Fang

John Woo's *The Killer* by Kenneth E. Hall

King Hu's *A Touch of Zen* by Stephen Teo

Mabel Cheung Yuen-ting's *An Autumn's Tale* by Stacilee Ford

Stanley Kwan's *Center Stage* by Mette Hjort

Tsui Hark's *Zu: Warriors From the Magic Mountain* by Andrew Schroeder

Wong Kar-wai's *Ashes of Time* by Wimal Dissanayake

Wong Kar-wai's *Happy Together* by Jeremy Tambling

YUEN WOO PING'S
Wing Chun

Sasha Vojković

香港大學出版社
HONG KONG UNIVERSITY PRESS

Hong Kong University Press
14/F Hing Wai Centre
7 Tin Wan Praya Road
Aberdeen
Hong Kong

ISBN 978-962-209-967-8

British Library Cataloguing-in-Publication Data
A catalogue record for this book is available from the British Library.

Secure on-line Ordering
http://www.hkupress.org

Printed and bound by Liang Yu Printing Factory Ltd., Hong Kong, China

Hong Kong University Press is honoured that Xu Bing, whose
art explores the complex themes of language across cultures,
has written the Press's name in his Square Word Calligraphy.
This signals our commitment to cross-cultural thinking and the
distinctive nature of our English-language books published in
China.

"At first glance, Square Word Calligraphy appears to be nothing
more unusual than Chinese characters, but in fact it is a new
way of rendering English words in the format of a square so they
resemble Chinese characters. Chinese viewers expect to be able
to read Square Word Calligraphy but cannot. Western viewers,
however are surprised to find they can read it. Delight erupts
when meaning is unexpectedly revealed."

— Britta Erickson, *The Art of Xu Bing*

Contents

Series Preface

The New Hong Kong Cinema came into existence under very special circumstances, during a period of social and political crisis resulting in a change of cultural paradigms. Such critical moments have produced the cinematic achievements of the early Soviet cinema, neorealism, the *nouvelle vague*, the German cinema in the 1970s and, we can now say, the recent Hong Kong cinema. If this cinema grew increasingly intriguing in the 1980s, after the announcement of Hong Kong's return to China, it was largely because it had to confront a new cultural and political space that was both complex and hard to define, where the problems of colonialism were overlaid with those of globalism in an uncanny way. Such uncanniness could not be caught through straight documentary or conventional history writing; it was left to the cinema to define it.

It does so by presenting to us an urban space that slips away if we try to grasp it too directly, a space that cinema coaxes into existence by whatever means at its disposal. Thus it is by eschewing a narrow idea of relevance and pursuing disreputable genres like melodrama, kung fu and the fantastic that cinema brings into view something else about the city which could otherwise be missed. One classic example is Stanley Kwan's *Rouge*, which draws on the unrealistic form of the ghost story to evoke something of the uncanniness of Hong Kong's urban space. It takes a ghost to catch a ghost.

In the New Hong Kong Cinema, then, it is neither the subject matter nor a particular set of generic conventions that is paramount. In fact, many Hong Kong films begin by following generic conventions but proceed to transform them. Such transformation of genre is also the transformation of a sense of place where all the rules have quietly and deceptively changed. It is this shifting sense of place, often expressed negatively and indirectly — but in the best work always rendered precisely in (necessarily) innovative images — that is decisive for the New Hong Kong Cinema.

Has the creative period of the New Hong Kong Cinema come to an end? However we answer the question, there is a need now to evaluate the achievements of Hong Kong cinema. During the last few years, a number of full-length books have appeared, testifying to the topicality of the subject. These books survey the field with varying degrees of success, but there is yet an almost complete lack of authoritative texts focusing in depth on individual Hong Kong films. This book series on the New Hong Kong Cinema is designed to fill this lack. Each volume will be written by a scholar/critic who will analyse each chosen film in detail and provide a critical apparatus for further discussion including filmography and bibliography.

Our objective is to produce a set of interactional and provocative readings that would make a self-aware intervention into modern Hong Kong culture. We advocate no one theoretical position; the authors will approach their chosen films from their own distinct points of vantage and interest. The aim of the series is to generate open-ended discussions of the selected films, employing diverse analytical strategies, in order to urge the readers towards self-reflective engagements with the films in particular and the Hong Kong cultural space in general. It is our hope that this series will contribute to the sharpening of Hong Kong culture's conceptions of itself.

In keeping with our conviction that film is not a self-enclosed signification system but an important cultural practice among similar others, we wish to explore how films both reflect and inflect culture. And it is useful to keep in mind that reflection of reality and reality of reflection are equally important in the understanding of cinema.

Ackbar Abbas
Wimal Dissanayake

Acknowledgements

First of all I would like to thank Mieke Bal for encouraging me to apply for the Y. K. Pao Postdoctoral Teaching Fellowship that enabled me to take part in the activities of the Center for Cultural Studies, and teach at the Division of Humanities of the Hong Kong University of Science and Technology. I am also thankful to Johannes Fabian and Thomas Elsaesser who helped to make this possible. I am especially grateful to Angelina Yee for her faith in me, and for her unconditional support, guidance, and friendship. It was a great privilege to work at the Division of Humanities where I had inspiring and productive interaction with the colleagues and students. There are so many people whose kindness I will never forget — Jowen Tung, Flora Fu, Virgil Ho, Yip Kaming, Karl Kao. It is equally difficult to express my thankfulness to the true "Hongkongers" Yip Man Fung and Yvonne Leung for their help with the activities of the Center for Cultural Studies, as well as Isha Ting, the best teaching assistant ever. This was a fantastic environment which provided the context for this book.

My first negotiations with Hong Kong University Press started with Ackbar Abbas and Wimal Disanayake and here, I need to express my deepest gratitude to Wimal Dissanayake for his engagement on the subject, his support, and thoughtful comments. From the outset I received encouragement and valuable help from the editors of Hong Kong University Press; Mina Kumar, at the very first stage; Colin Day in the crucial stage of finalizing the book; and most recently, from Michael Duckworth. Many, many thanks to them all for the interest they expressed in my work.

1

Yuen Woo Ping and the Art of Empowering Female Characters

The Art of Countering Dominant Structures of Meaning

Yuen Woo Ping's films do not conform to the traditional notions of film art and stylistic innovation, and his status as author is not so self-evident. Unlike the "New Wavers," the cosmopolitan filmmakers who rejuvenated Hong Kong's production framework by bringing Western standards to the industry, Yuen Woo Ping, like Sammo Hung and Corey Yuen Kuei, is a studio-trained director who began his career in the late 1970s by reviving the martial arts film.[1] Although Yuen is acknowledged as one of the filmmakers who introduced comic elements into the kung fu genre,[2] he is not perceived as an author who has redefined the genre in the manner of Tsui Hark (*Butterfly Murders/Die bian/Dip bin,* 1979) or Patrick Tam (*The Sword/Ming jian/Ming jim,* 1980), the directors of the Hong Kong New Wave, or the directors who represent the New Hong Kong Cinema such as Wong Kar-wai (*Ashes of Time/Dong xie xi du/Dung che sai duk,* 1994).[3]

In contrast to these art film "literate" directors,[4] who sought ways to de/re-construct the hero and give an "artistic" twist to the martial arts genre, Yuen is better known as the "action director"[5] who sought new ways to keep the action genre alive through his capacity to make the characters leap, fly, and defy both gravity and common sense. In fact, the international recognition he acquired several years ago came through his work as action director/choreographer, in globally popular films such as *The Matrix* (Andy and Larry Wachowski, 1999) and its sequel *The Matrix Revolutions* (2003), *Crouching Tiger, Hidden Dragon/Wo hu cang long/Ngo fu chong lung* (Ang Lee, 2000) and most recently through Quentin Tarantino's *Kill Bill* volumes 1 (2003) and 2 (2004).[6]

Unlike Yuen, filmmakers with similar career paths, enjoyed author status in critical writing, such as the above-mentioned Sammo Hung, or Lau Kar Leung, who I will discuss in subsequent chapters. All three of them followed the trajectory of the so-called studio-trained director, which implies that they started as stuntmen and bit players, advanced to the status of action choreographers, and were finally offered the chance to direct their own films. The specificity of this type of filmmaker is that, even though at one point he acquired the position of director, he continued to be involved as action choreographer on his own projects and/or the projects of his colleagues. As is the case concretely (although not only) with Yuen, as mentioned above, these Hong Kong directors are engaged in big budget Hollywood productions.

In Chapter 4 I will say more about why it is difficult to separate Yuen's persona as director/author from his position as action choreographer. What is more, the idiosyncrasies of his filmic universe in many ways converge with the preoccupations of his colleagues. Since the central interest of this study is Yuen Woo Ping's film *Wing Chun*, I will point to the films from his body of work that can be taken as exemplary of a certain type of universe. More precisely, I will focus on his kung fu comedies that most prominently demonstrate a consistent preoccupation with subverting the interests of the martial arts tradition, implying in the first instance that instead of dignified male heroes who fight against foreign intruders or corrupt authorities, in Yuen's films we frequently encounter problematic, weak, or ridiculous men and strong women. In spite of the fact that kung fu comedy is invested in subverting the interests of the martial arts tradition, it has also been noted that this sub-genre belongs to the homosocial, macho world. In this environment women are also depicted as nagging or grotesque figures, but they are granted the physical and verbal skills that enables them to spar (but not exclusively) with their spouses (Hunt 2003). This is, in any case, a specificity of Hong Kong cinema, and a selection of films from Yuen's filmic universe is an occasion to shed additional light on this cinema.

Although his films feature predominantly male action heroes epitomized in the image of the famous martial arts master Wong Fei Hung/Huang Fei Hong (the most popular version is the comical one interpreted by Jackie Chan),[7] they offer us some of the most extraordinary action women in the history of cinema, culminating with the legendary martial arts heroine Wing Chun. My interest in writing this monograph that coheres around Yuen's 1993 kung fu comedy *Wing Chun/Yong Chun* comes from my long term fascination with Hong Kong cinema's tradition of female warriors. *Wing Chun* is a rare example of a filmic text that functions according to "the Law of the Woman," and it offers a painfully simplistic, yet incredibly empowering (albeit imaginary) solution to the (far from resolved) crisis of femininity. We will see that the balance of this fictional world is achieved across three levels, each of which is closely dependent on the working of female subjectivity: 1) female action, 2) female interaction, and 3) female personification of the highest narrational authority. The restructuring of subjectivity is closely tied with the re-shaping of the fabula, whereby a history/ legend about a woman warrior becomes intertwined with contemporary concerns with female empowerment. The fixing of the problem on the level of the fictional world coincides with the re-definition of female subjectivity.

Speaking of the representation of femininity in Yuen's films, I am not only referring to the women warriors who can "save the world," albeit by forging a partnership with a male hero as in his *Tai-Chi Master/Tai ji zhang san feng* (1993) or *Iron Monkey/Shao nian Huan Fei Hong zhi tie ma liu/Siu nin Wong Fei Hung ji tit ma lau* (1993), nor am I alluding to the woman who can set the fictional world into balance single-handedly as is the case with *Wing Chun*. Yuen's films such as *Drunken Master/Zui quan/Jui kuen (1978)*, *Dance of the Drunk Mantis/Nan bei zui quan/Laam bak chui kuen* (1979), *Dreadnaught/Yong zhe wu ju/Yung che miu gui (1981)*, or *Drunken Tai-Chi/Xiao tai chi/Siu taai gik* (1984) feature amazingly skilled yet utterly common female characters in supporting roles — middle-aged mothers, sisters, or wives who can stand up for themselves in the most spectacular ways. What is additionally noteworthy about the examples of films that feature these women of action is that they offer us insight into diverse faces of femininity, from the submissive and the oppressed to the emancipated. In spite of the fact that some of these female characters have no proper function in propelling the events, and even if the exhibition of their fighting skills is at times just a set piece inserted into a seemingly simplistic story, we need to interpret these actions in terms of their critical value. These women's actions are significant because, as mentioned above, they almost regularly demonstrate a female capacity to fight against verbal, physical, or any other kind of abuse.

In that respect, I will suggest that Yuen Woo Ping's "art" should be observed in terms of its subversive function, a view that is inspired by Gilles Deleuze and Felix Guattari's writings on the deterritorializing function of art. I am referring here to their concepts from *Anti-Oedipus* and *A Thousand Plateaus: Capitalism and Schizophrenia,* and in Chapter 2 I will take recourse to Deleuze's writings on film, specifically, his work *Movement-Image* (Deleuze 1983). Deleuze is a key figure in postmodern thought and one of the first philosophers who wrote about film. While traditional film theory treats film as a series of static photographic images, Deleuze argues that film consists of movement-images and time-images. In the books he wrote with Guattari he puts forward an anti-Freudian position as well as the ideas of the micropolitics of power. At the center of interest are (conceptual means that could theoretically forge) open and non-repressive societies. In *A Thousand Plateaus*, for example, they introduce concepts such as deterritorialization, becoming, bodies without organs and line of flight (Deleuze and Guattari 1996). Each of these concepts alludes to the non-hierarchical, two-way relations of different forms that affect the politics of identity. Via these ideas and concepts, an identity is propagated that is in a constant process of becoming; at stake is the conceptual space where meanings flow freely. I will examine Yuen's kung fu comedies as examples of the "art of empowering women and subverting patriarchal authorities," and I will argue that these principally commercial genre films (that cannot be categorized as "art [house] films")[8] should be discussed in terms of their deterritorializing function, or more precisely, their capacity to forge an empowering image of femininity. What this concretely means in terms of Yuen's body of work is that I will discuss the idiosyncrasies of his persona as filmmaker not only in relation to the employment of cinematic devices in his films or the organization of space and time;[9] rather, I will place my main emphasis on the narrative representation of issues such as gender and power/authority.[10]

In my previous work I have discussed concrete Hong Kong films in terms of the "art of countering territorial regimes," and I have taken this in a double sense, as connected to Hong Kong as an actual physical territory, but also in terms of the production of meaning.[11] I have argued that the art of specific Hong Kong films is interdependent with the countering of certain regimes of signs. As far as the study of Yuen's filmic universe is concerned (and *Wing Chun* is the model example), the countering of territorial regimes implies also opposing the structures of meaning which are dependent on the cultural fixations, norms, and rules that govern the construction of the regressive image of femininity based initially on the assumption that women are passive, whereas men are active. The countering of such fixations involves the connection between the cinematic representation of gender and narrative.

It is important to point out that narrative representation is not only determined by the process of cinematic storytelling/narration, but also by a certain mode of cultural expression that informs the film's fabula. The actions these women are able to perform have to do with the connection between the narrative and the rules and norms that regulate what kind of female character is imaginable and conceivable. This implies that the "art of empowering women" is also bound up with a specific cultural imaginary. Speaking generally of Hong Kong films that feature fabulas populated with female heroes, it is possible to argue that these films work contrary to the laws of common sense that govern the social imagination of Western traditions. The viewing pleasure derives from the exhilarating action scenes and the super human skills of the characters such as Wing Chun, but at the same time the sense of empowerment emanates from the fictional worlds/fabulas predicated on specific conventions and practices.

History as Science Fiction

According to Clifford Geertz, even though common sense seems to be about the mere matter-of-fact apprehension of reality, or down to earth colloquial judgments, we have to consider the fact that the diversity of artistic expressions stems from the variety of conceptions we have about the ways things are (Geertz 1983). In Geertz's view, vernacular characterizations of *what happens* are connected to vernacular imaginings of *what can*. Geertz brings forward the notion of "legal sensibility" implying that stories and imaginings are contingent on a law; this law is rejoined to the other cultural formations of human life such as morals, art, technology, science, religion, division of labor, and history. Traditional Chinese society was male-dominated and men were regarded as superior to women. Confucian teaching codified this hierarchy.[12] Although the feminine element is so essential in the philosophical sense (particularly in Taoist thought, for it is interwoven with the masculine element), such a balance of forces cannot be found and confirmed in the actual position of women in everyday life, in traditionally patriarchal Chinese society.

In spite of female subordination in daily life, the stories of women warriors remained alive, and remarkably, women play a heroic role to an extent that is without parallel in European or Anglo-American action-adventure films. Apart from Taoism and Confucianism, when it comes to the question of social and cultural formations that regulate what women can do, *Wing Chun* reminds us of the third dominant religion in China — Buddhism. Since the way towards transcendence under Buddhism was equally applicable to both men and women, it is not strange that this would emerge in films.

For example, Wing Chun's teacher of martial arts and the highest narratorial authority in the film is a Buddhist nun; this *can happen* because in Confucian China, Buddhism and Taoism acknowledge, at least theoretically, women's equality with men. There is an egalitarian principle at work, where both men and women can achieve spiritual fulfillment. Quite understandably, then, Wing Chun could find refuge in a Buddhist temple and learn kung fu from a Buddhist woman.

Therefore, the fact that women are elaborated as skilled fighters is related to the specificities of the genre incorporated into the process of cinematic storytelling, but it is the specific vision of the film, a vision that exceeds the level of the fictional world that determines what kind of female subject is conceivable and which actions she can perform. The intelligent women fighters, women who are knowing subjects the types of female characters that can be found in Beijing Opera, martial arts novels, or the traditional Chinese stories of the fantastic and the supernatural — are dependent on the norms that circulate within Chinese cultural heritage.[13] One prototype that has served as a model for many Chinese girls and women who wished to abandon a strictly feminine role and gain access to the political sphere is Hua Mulan (Fa Mulan in Cantonese) the heroine of the Five Dynasties (420–588). A legendary figure, she has remained famous (and was even re-imagined in a Hollywood movie) because of an anonymous poet who sang her praise in the famous "Song of Mulan."

One of the most indicative examples from the tradition of women warriors is the film *The Temple of the Red Lotus/Jiang hu qi xia/Tsan hong tsu* (Chui Chang Wang/Hung Hsu Tseng, 1965) in which all the female members of the family are trained in martial arts, including Lianzhu/Lian Chu (Chin Ping), the central female character in the film.

Still 1.1   Still 1.2

Stills 1.1, 1.2 In *The Temple of the Red Lotus* (Chui Chang Wang/Hung Hsu Tseng, 1965), the mother reminds her daughter of the daily kung fu lesson with her father.

On Lianzhu's wedding night, her mother enters the newlywed's bedchamber and whispers something mysterious to her (Still 1.1). The young husband (Jimmy Wang Yu) is unpleasantly surprised when he learns that the mother has reminded the daughter of her daily kung fu lesson with her father (Still 1.2). In this film the grandmother (Lam Jing) is portrayed as the highest authority of the family. This is underscored with her dragonhead staff with a bell attached to it; in the film, her presence is established metonymically via the head of the staff and the sound of the bell (Still 1.3).

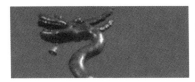

Still 1.3   The grandmother's authority is metonymically marked through her dragonhead staff with a bell attached to it.

When the young couple wants to leave Jin Castle, a family rule is applied — they have to fight their way out. Since the men are not in the castle, Lianzhu and her husband Wu have to fight a series of women: Lianzhu's sister-in-law (Stills 1.4, 1.5); Lianzhu's aunt (Stills 1.6, 1.7); Lianzhu's mother (Stills 1.8, 1.9); Lianzhu's grandmother (Stills 1.10, 1.11).

Still 1.4   Still 1.5

Stills 1.4, 1.5   A series of women try to prevent the young couple from leaving the family castle. One of them is Lianzhu's sister-in-law.

Still 1.6

Still 1.7

Stills 1.6, 1.7   Lianzhu's aunt follows.

Still 1.8

Still 1.9

Stills 1.8, 1.9   The next one is Lianzhu's mother.

Still 1.10

Still 1.11

Stills 1.10, 1.11   Finally, the young couple has to confront the grandmother, the head of the family.

The young couple overcomes each barrier not by outshining the martial arts expertise of their opponents but through pleading and crying. The grandmother, however, is not as merciful, and since Lianzhu has greater knowledge of kung fu than her husband Wu, she engages in a duel with her grandmother while Wu waits on the other side of the river.[14] Ultimately, the grandmother too spares their lives, and soon Lianzhu and Wu are on their way.

There is one female authority, however, who is on an even higher level; this is the Red Lady Sword (Ivy Ling Po), the best fighter of all. She acts as Lianzhu's and Wu's guardian angel, coming to their rescue on several occasions. Her superior position is indicated quite literally in the film; her point of vision and action is "from above" (Still 1.12); that is, she appears on the rooftops or hills (Stills 1.13, 1.14). The Red Lady watches over those who need help, and through her effective interventions she controls the outcome of events.

Still 1.12

Still 1.13

Still 1.14

Stills 1.12–1.14   The Red Lady Sword is the highest authority, positioned literally above everyone.

Referring to the traditional examples of women warriors, we have to recall the famous female clan of the Yang family, with its several generations of women generals and, as in *The Temple of the Red Lotus*, with the grandmother as the grand matriarch at the top of the pyramid. According to the legend, the Yang women took part in battles in order to avenge their husbands and fathers, the male warriors of the family, or to serve the country in place of the male members, who had all lost their lives in battles (Still 1.15).

Still 1.15 *Ladies of the Great Yang Family*, from the Beijing opera classic. The grandmother is in the front.

Drama historian A. C. Scott describes the Beijing opera matriarchs (*laodan*) as "halting in step but firm in spirit, forceful in expression and emotional in their grief, they are constantly concerned with the honor of family life and the unity of the clan" (1983: 125).

In the history of Hong Kong cinema, one of the most famous grandmothers is Chin Tsi Ang, the actual grandmother of the famous Hong Kong director, actor, and action choreographer Sammo Hung. Chin Tsi Ang is one of the first female martial arts heroines in a film (Stills 1.16, 1.17); she starred in the 1930 film *The Lady Sword Fighter of Jiangnan/Huangjiang nüxia* (Shang Guanwu). [15]

Still 1.16

Still 1.17

Stills 1.16, 1.17   Chin Tsi Ang, one of the earliest women of action, in *The Lady Sword Fighter of Jiangnan* (Shang Guanwu, 1930).

The characters and stories that we can find in the traditions of Hong Kong cinema, an example of which is the legend of Wing Chun are bound up with cultural and social framings, options, and constraints. The emergence of powerful female characters is strongly connected to the stories that occurred "a long, long time ago in a universe far, far away," but this is not the case of a generic clash between fairy tale and science fiction that infers a temporal disjunction and a past that is yet to come.[16] If we recall some of the most famous action heroines in the Hollywood films — the characters such as Princess Leia from the *Star Wars* series, Ellen Ripley from the *Alien* series, or Sarah Connor from the *Terminator* sequel, we will notice that the first and the most important difference between the Hong Kong and the Hollywood heroines is that the latter come from the future.[17] The reason for this is because no narrative justification could be found to situate them in the past (or the present).[18]

Discussions on the reinvention of femininity through the action genre as it is manifested especially in contemporary Hollywood have occasionally been geared toward the female warriors of Hong Kong cinema who appeared on the big screens many decades earlier than their Hollywood counterparts.[19] One of the reasons for this, as it has been pointed out, is that the diverse traditions of Hong Kong cinema permit different sorts of characters and not just the main protagonists, to be fighters. In Yuen Woo Ping's film *Drunken Master*, for example, there need not be a special narrative justification for a middle-aged mother to engage in a martial arts combat with the young Wong Fei Hung who has threatened her daughter's chastity. In terms of Hong Kong cinema, this is an act of common sense. We will see that in the narratives from Yuen Woo Ping's universe the action is set in the past but the women seem to be emancipated in ways unimaginable in Western traditions. In these Hong Kong films, almost literally, history comes to figure as science fiction.[20]

Deleuze and Guattari state that it is through creative fabulation "that hidden universes are drawn out of the shadow by a beam of light", but I would add that in the case of Hong Kong cinema it is in the first instance the cultural imaginary that conditions the emergence of alternative universes and fabulas (Deleuze and Guattari 1994: 171). These fabulas put pressure on the traditional feminist theory, which relies on a psychoanalytic framework, for they bring forth unexpected connections, transformations, and lines of flight from the dominant structures of meaning.[21] The universe of Wing Chun is an example of such a fictional world, because here, as we will find, desire is not regulated through oedipal structures or the Law of the Father; the law at work in this filmic narrative is the "Law of Wing Chun."[22] What makes *Wing Chun* so different from other martial arts films that feature female warriors is the fact that this film departs from the paternal line that generally governs the narrative structure of kung fu film. Here, the master/pupil relationship is established between two women, which is practically an exception even in Hong Kong cinema.[23]

At this point I would like to emphasize that, in a broader sense, the notion of an "imaginary solution" can be taken as analogous to Deleuze and Guattari's idea of creative fabulation. More precisely, I am using this notion to underscore the capacity of narrative to propel symbolic communication and to point to the urgency of (re)discovering and (re)inventing myths, histories, and fabulas, for they have the power to shape and promote a certain vision of the world — or to put it in Deleuzian terms, to create and enable lines of flight from territoriality of semiotic regimes.[24]

Speed, Rest, Sensation, and Deterritorialization

The reinvention of femininity and masculinity through the action genre involved cases such as men being turned into a spectacle as well as women becoming both masculinized and *musculinized*.[25] In contrast to the Hollywood examples, the women warriors in Hong Kong action films cannot be described as *musculinized,* for their bodies are not muscled and man-like even when they have a masculine appearance. Even though Wing Chun's aunt tells her she has lost everything except the fists, Wing Chun doesn't really display the masculine features of the characters such as Sarah Connor in *Terminator 2* or Ripley in *Alien Resurrection.* Her "masculinization" can rather be attributed to the Chinese cultural imaginary.

I am referring in the first place to the "body of Tao," the Taoist priority given to the human body over social and cultural systems. We can trace this tradition in Beijing opera, which, had such a profound influence on the martial arts and swordplay genre of Hong Kong cinema, including the kung fu comedy. Traditionally, the "masculinization" of female fighters in Hong Kong cinema is not perceived as a problem, and it does not bring the character's femininity into question. Their masculinity does not presuppose the loss of femininity, for their character entails duality, two in one, as is typically the case in Beijing opera. This type of female character is called *wudan,* and it designates a cross-dressing woman of action who maintains her feminine appeal (A. C. Scott 1983).

Interestingly, until the very end of the film, Wing Chun is dressed as a man. On the one hand, the film draws on the tradition of female cross-dressing, but in this kung fu comedy cross-dressing also evokes contemporary play with gender, in particular the idea of gender as performance. This is especially evident in scenes where Wing Chun is confused with a man; this can be perceived as subversive confusion, and we could say that in such instances cross-dressing provokes, in Judith Butler's sense, gender trouble. For Butler, gender trouble has positive connotations, as does the parodying of gender through cross-dressing (Butler 1993). Even though cross-dressing is a cultural stereotype and Wing Chun dressed in male attire can fool everyone, including her childhood sweetheart, we know that she is of the female sex. Therefore, Wing Chun's tender interaction with another woman (in a scene that I will discuss in Chapter 2) can inevitably be perceived in today's context as "queer." Her "queerness" points to the unstable structure of gender, and it has a deterritorializing effect. These strategies were pushed to phenomenal extremes in films directed or produced by Tsui Hark starring Brigitte Lin, for example, *Peking Opera Blues/Do ma daan* (Tsui Hark, 1986), *Swordsman II/Xiao ao jiang hu zhi Dong Fang Bu Bai* (Ching Siu Tong, 1992), and *The East Is Red/Dung Fong Bat Baai: Fung wan joi hei* (Ching Siu Tung, Raymond Lee, 1992). The reason, of course, that Lin acquired the status of a filmic gender-bending persona is the cultural heritage, or rather, the tradition of cross-dressing that was imported into film from Chinese opera.

Due to her "male appearance" throughout the film, Wing Chun needs to win back her female organism, to put it in Deleuze's and Guattari's terms. She needs to affirm herself both as a *woman* and *the best fighter*. Even though she ultimately appears looking like a woman (implying she is dressed and made up as a woman) this is not how her femaleness, her female authority is ultimately established. She reclaims her subjectivity by inventing her own fighting method, hence, by *fighting like a woman*. Winning back the female organism, that is, "becoming-woman" can also be understood in relation to Deleuze's and Guattari's idea of molar politics, or rather their assertion that "it is indispensable for women to conduct a molar politics with a view of winning back their own organism, their own history, their own subjectivity" (Deleuze and Guattari 1996: 275–6). This molar politics needs to be regarded within their view that all becomings are molecular including becoming-woman. According to Deleuze and Guattari, becoming-woman is more than just imitating or assuming the female form, at stake is the capacity to emit particles "that enter the relation of movement and rest, or the zone of proximity, of a microfemininity [...]" (275–6). This coincides with Butler's assertions on the artificiality of gender, implying that gender marks performance rather than identity.

Maxine Hong Kingston is one of the writers who stressed the importance of telling stories about becoming-woman, more specifically of becoming-woman warrior. In her fictional biography, Kingston invents a story of how she herself became a woman warrior, but first she tells stories of women warriors, recounted by her mother. She tells of Fa Mulan, the girl who took her father's place in a battle, and of the woman who invented white crane boxing:

> It was a woman who invented white crane boxing only two hundred years ago. She was already an expert pole fighter, daughter of a teacher trained at the Shaolin temple, where there lived an order of fighting monks. She was combing her hair one morning when a white crane alighted outside her window. She teased it with her pole, which it pushed aside with a soft brush of its wing. Amazed, she dashed outside and tried to knock the crane off its perch. It snapped her pole in two. Recognizing the presence of a great power, she asked the spirit of the white crane if it would teach her to fight. It answered with a cry that white crane boxers imitate today. Later the bird returned as an old man and he guided her boxing for many years. Thus she gave the world a new martial art. (Hong Kingston 1977: 19)

In this socio-cultural imaginary, a woman *can* give the world a martial art, which conversely implies that through a martial art she can confirm her female identity. Speaking of becoming in terms of this filmic narrative, I would suggest that Wing Chun's microfemininity is most prominently expressed through her martial arts, through the actual relation of speed and slowness so brilliantly choreographed by Yuen Woo Ping and magnificently executed by

Michelle Yeoh. In this context, Yeoh's own "becoming" is equally important, for she has transformed from a beauty queen into an authentic female fighter whose bravery can match the heroic stunts of Jackie Chan. Yeoh wasn't trained in martial arts, but thanks to her perseverance and audacity, her action scenes became as authentic as those of the best male fighters. While the fabula of the legendary heroine Wing Chun conditions the sense of empowerment echoed in contemporary women of action, Yeoh's speed and slowness expressed through her ability to perform most of her own stunt work conditions conversely Wing Chun's microfemininity. Wing Chun's character-image depends on the narrative drive of an action cinema, but the fact that it is a female character that can execute the action through the dynamic of speed and slowness creates the unique sense relation that I have described as the sense of empowerment. By means of this sense relation, Wing Chun's character-image acquires the status of the empowerment-image.

Keeping in mind concerns about the narrative representation of gender and power, for the purpose of the analysis of *Wing Chun,* in Chapter 2 I will introduce the critical narratological approach; what is crucial is the interest in what is told, how it is told, and who takes part in the process of the telling.[26] The concrete filmic narrative will thus be observed as a network of semiotic events. The deterritorializing function of Yuen Woo Ping's art will in the first instance be traced precisely through an examination of the meaning making process. This type of narratological analysis will enable us to draw conclusions about the "creative" aspect of fabulations and indicate the ways in which they counter specific regimes of signs.

I will consider two levels, or rather the interaction between the formal elements/filmic devices (as these are related to the aspects of cinematic storytelling), and the elements of narrative (the fabula). The examination of the elements and aspects of narrative in *Wing Chun* in Chapters 2 and 3 will demonstrate that the art of countering territorial regimes of signs pertains to both levels. The studying of these processes will enable us to establish the ways in which legal sensibility affects narrative representation. Keeping with the aims of this study, ascertaining *what can* will provide insight into the ways in which narrative, as interrelated with legal sensibility, affects the representation of gender and power.

Since the fabulas of Yuen's films feature diverse women of action another vital issue is how their character-images are constructed. As mentioned earlier, in Yuen's body of work we encounter middle-aged, old, or even fat women of action who can teach the men a lesson; all these women move so fast that their actions are at times practically imperceptible. Deleuze and Guattari assert that "knowing how to age does not mean remaining young, it means extracting from one's age the particles, the speed and slowness, the flows that constitute the youth of that age" (277). Evidently, some of these women of action have aged and yet in a quite literal way they embody the speed and slowness that constitute the youth of their (older) age. Their ability to oscillate between speed and slowness is what gives them the power to counter patriarchal fixations and to offer imaginary solutions to the crisis of femininity.

When discussing movement and rest, and speed and slowness, the inevitable pair of complementaries that we can add is yin and yang — the Taoist principle of equal exchange between activity and passivity. Yin and yang are the two fundamental phases of Tao's action; they serve to designate cold and hot, moon and sun, soft and hard, feminine and masculine, death and life. Their complementary opposition exists in everything, and their alternation is the first law of Chinese cosmology: when yin reaches its apex, it changes into yang, and vice versa (Schipper 1993). This reminds us that the dynamic of exchange of complementary particles that generate the process of "becoming" can in this case also be seen as intertwined with the specificities of a concrete cultural imaginary.

The analysis of Yuen's filmic universe in Chapter 4 shows that the inadequate men in particular have repercussions on the construction of the image of femininity in his films. I map out the context from which Yuen's films emerged, and I also compare his career path with those of Sammo Hung and Lau Kar Leung. In relation to the representation of women the men are principally elaborated as negative characters; they prove to be weaker and less capable, including the fathers, who often have no authority. In *Wing Chun*, even the chief of the bandits, who is an excellent fighter, is defeated in the end. In contrast to the films of the late 1960s and early 1970s, where the inadequate (male) authority is implied mostly through the foreign invaders or through corrupt government officials, and where women warriors take part in battles alongside their male counterparts, in the kung fu comedies such as *Wing Chun,* the fathers or male authorities need not be foreign or corrupt to be mocked. The plethora of inadequate men who appear in Yuen's films most blatantly spells out the urgency of giving both patriarchy and paternity a face.[27] Again, Deleuze's and Guattari's concepts are relevant here: apart from the concept of "de/re-territorialization" and "becoming" as related to narrative representation, I will additionally introduce the concept of "the body without organs" (hereafter BwO in this volume).

Since there is no ready-made poetics that can incorporate all the gravity defying creatures of Hong Kong cinema, including the female characters in the films of Yuen Woo Ping, I will work with a *poietics*. Poietics entails sensitivity and openness to an ongoing process and a multiplicity of connections, rather than a fixed set of rules; it can be seen as a fluctuating and a fluid manual, the type of manual inspired by Deleuze and Guattari's ideas on art. The term is derived from the Aristotelian notion of *poiesis,* implying creation or production. In accordance with these ideas, the analyses in this study will focus on the art of countering territorial regimes (the art of empowering female characters being the most prominent example) involving both the elements of the fabula and the aspects of the story. Bearing in mind the discussions of the first four chapters, in the concluding chapter I focus on the ways in which these fabulations that generate a sense of female empowerment put pressure on traditional film theory (above all, feminist film theory) and on the dominant theories of cinematic narration. The analyses ultimately help us establish the ways in which deterritorializations and becomings from this cinema of alternative fictional worlds become intertwined with dominant concerns regarding gender and sexuality, subjectivity, and trans/cultural memory.

2

Structuring the Narrative: Becoming "Wing Chun"

The Film's Fabula: A Mode of Cultural Expression

The type of narratological analysis that I propose for the study of *Wing Chun* implicates first of all the three levels that a narrative comprises — the text, the story, and the fabula. A narrative text is a text in which an agent relates — tells — a story in a particular medium such as film (Bal 1997). To follow Mieke Bal's working definition of narrative, a story is a fabula that is presented in a certain manner, and a fabula is a series of logically and chronologically related events. The story determines a specific rhetoric that has direct implications on the epistemological value of the text; the way the events are ordered into a story, the way a fabula is framed or re-framed through the process of storytelling enables us to draw conclusions about the concerns that are embedded into the fictional world.[1]

As viewers, we are able to re-construct the fabula only in the very end, after it has been presented in some way as a story, and thus we tend to disregard the fact that fabulas of narrative texts are dependent on the concerns derived from the outer world. Or, as Bal explains, fabulas make describable a segment of reality that is broader than that of the narrative text itself (Bal 1997). The fabula of *Wing Chun* confirms this: according to the legend, Yim Wing Chun learned the art of kung fu from a Buddhist nun by the name of Ng Mui who was famous for her skill at fighting on top of the "plum blossom poles."[2] Hers is a southern style of fighting founded on direct, close-contact fighting, a combination of straight and intercepting lines and deflecting arcs. The style was named "Wing Chun" after Ng Mui's female pupil. As the legend goes, Wing Chun's beauty attracted the attention of a local bully. He tried to force Wing Chun to marry him and his persistent threats became a source of worry to her and her father. Ng Mui learned of this and took pity on Wing Chun. She agreed to teach Wing Chun some fighting techniques so that she could protect herself. Wing Chun followed Ng Mui to the mountains, where she trained night and day until she had mastered the techniques. In this place of exile, Wing Chun redefined herself, as did the heroine from *A Touch of Zen/Hsia nu/Hap lui,* for example, when she retreated to the Buddhist temple in King Hu's 1969 masterpiece. Hidden away in the mountains, she was taught swordplay skills by Buddhist monks. The fabulas of these films echo the structures of meaning on the extradiegetic level. An example from literature is Maxine Hong Kingston's novel *Woman Warrior: Memoirs of a Girlhood Among Ghosts*, which tells of a young woman who goes away to learn kung fu, and then returns as a general, riding at the head of an army of men to defend her village from a monstrous horde. When Wing Chun returns to her village she challenges the bully to a fight and defeats him.

This myth of emancipation of the female Shaolin Temple student is a pre-text to Yuen Woo Ping's 1994 film *Wing Chun.* The events that occur in Yuen's film take place after that, continuing Wing Chun's story past the legend. This implies that the film deals with a possible narrative/fabula/history, or a succession of events that could have occurred after Wing Chun returned home from her training and established herself as an authority in the martial arts. The pre-text, that is, the legend, conditions the premise (of the filmic narrative) that in a seventeenth-century village in China the best fighter is a woman by the name of Wing Chun. Constantly engaged in kung fu training and, dressed in male attire, she seems to have sacrificed her feminine side to sustain her position as the kung fu expert and a protector of the people. She lives with her aunt, who runs a bean curd business. Although the past problem (of power and gender) is solved, a new, yet similar, pressure is put on her female identity. In the course of the film, the tale about the woman being pressured into marriage repeats itself illustrating for us that history, the pre-text, is mirrored in the film's story.

Telling the Story: Re-constructing the Fabula

In this fictional world, Wing Chun is not the prey of the implied villain; instead, she represents an entity that can bring law and order to her community. In Yuen's *Wing Chun*, the prey of the villain is Charmy (Catherine Hung Yan), the young and attractive widow who would have had to sell herself after her husband's death if Wing Chun and her entrepreneurial aunt Fung, alias Stinky Soya Bean Cube (Yuen King Tan), had not taken her under their wing. Just as the old narrative is reflected in the new one — a villain terrorizing a young woman — Wing Chun's history is reflected in Charmy's present circumstances.

Setting Charmy free from the bandits' fortress is not the only difficulty Wing Chun has to face in this narrative. The other problem she needs to resolve is related to the crisis of gender further complicated by Wing Chun's identity crisis. The confusion man/woman and the doubling of Wing Chun in Charmy reminds us of this. To provide the answer to the seemingly transparent question, "Who is Wing Chun?" we first have to trace the structuring of the narrative where history is figuring as present.

Charmy joins the family business and starts working as a salesgirl in Aunt Fung's bean curd shop, which is the job Wing Chun had before she became a famous kung fu fighter. To give a boost to the soya bean curd business, Aunt Fung gives Charmy the pretty clothes Wing Chun once wore when she was a young girl selling bean curd. She also teaches her the techniques of seducing men into buying bean curd. In regard to this, Charmy can be understood as a version of Wing Chun's former self, implying that Wing Chun is doubled in Charmy. The sight of Charmy in her "feminine" clothes triggers memories and self-reflection. This is underscored through a very overt filmic sign: as Wing Chun gazes at Charmy's new appearance, the camera zooms to a closer view of her distressed face (Stills 2.1–2.4).

Still 2.1

Still 2.2

Still 2.3

Still 2.4

Stills 2.1–2.4   Wing Chun is mirrored in Charmy as the new Miss Soya Bean.

The new image of Charmy, then, enables us to catch a glimpse of Wing Chun's image from the past, as it were. In contrast to the present situation, where due to her male attire, she is regularly mistaken for a man, back then, we can conclude, her female identity was transparent. Just as Wing Chun in the past, Charmy, a young woman of striking beauty, becomes the target of a villain. This time it is not the local bully who causes trouble, but a gang of bandits. In the current narrative Wing Chun acts as Charmy's savior, but since Charmy is also structurally figuring as Wing Chun (pretty; young; "Miss Soya Bean"; target of a villain) the rescuing of Charmy will condition conversely Wing Chun's own "rescue." More precisely, through the ultimate reaffirmation of Wing Chun's authority her femininity needs to be reclaimed. Therefore, the structuring of subjectivity is in the first instance related to the process of storytelling, where history/the fabula appears to be repeating itself. By having to face the villain once again, Wing Chun is given another chance to redefine herself. Again, at stake is the relation between power and gender. She was forced to marry in the past, and now again, the chief bandit Flying Monkey warns her that if she loses the fight she will be his wife.

Saving Charmy: Rescuing Wing Chun's Subjectivity

As we learn from the film, Wing Chun had a childhood sweetheart named Leung Pok To, who has now returned to the village and is looking for her. Pok To is played by the famed martial artist, actor, director, and filmmaker Donnie Yen and it is of course comical that in this film his martial arts skills are weaker than those of Wing Chun (played by actress Michelle Yeoh). We are well aware of his status as a martial arts expert and hence the comic element comes from extratextual and intertextual information. Upon his arrival he goes first to the bean curd shop and startled by Charmy's attractive appearance, Pok To mistakes her for Wing Chun. When Wing Chun arrives on the scene Pok To wrongly concludes that Wing Chun is Charmy's male lover (Stills 2.5–2.7).

Still 2.5

Still 2.6

Still 2.7

Stills 2.5–2.7 Wing Chun's cross-dressing as a cultural marker is turned into subversive gender confusion.

As Wing Chun caringly wipes the sweat off Charmy's face and Charmy responds with the same gesture, we notice that a "special bond" has already been established between the two women. The scene can be taken as a provocation of gender trouble whereby female cross-dressing as a cultural marker is turned into subversive confusion. What additionally triggers laughs then is the "queer" interaction between the two women.

Considering that ten years have passed since they last saw each other, Wing Chun also fails to recognize her sweetheart, and as in a comedy of errors, in one of the subsequent scenes she even mistakes him for one of the bandits. Charmy is ignorant of the actual state of affairs and regards Pok To as a very promising suitor. When Charmy realizes that Pok To has made the wrong assumption she wants to clarify the matter, but Wing Chun prevents her from disclosing her identity. She does not see the point in revealing her identity to Pok To for he seems to be interested in the "other Wing Chun" (i.e. Charmy). Even though she is hurt, she selflessly steps back and keeps up the pretense that Charmy is "Wing Chun." Her practical aunt tries to dissuade her because in her view Charmy is the "enemy," but Wing Chun does not agree; when Charmy is abducted, Wing Chun sets off to the bandits' fortress to help her female friend. On her way, she unexpectedly encounters Pok To who is also planning to rescue "Wing Chun."

As the two of them sit by the fire, they start talking about "Wing Chun," who is in danger of becoming the bride of one of the bandits. Pok To evokes the past and starts retelling fragments from the legend/pretext; he says that Wing Chun was forced to marry once before. Wing Chun dovetails to Pok To's story and starts recounting her own experiences in the third person. Just as Siu Lin from Yuen Woo Ping's *The Tai-Chi Master* and Miss Ho from his *Iron Monkey* (which I discuss in Chapter 4), Wing Chun was a very different woman in the past. She tells Pok To that "Miss Soya Bean" had to learn kung fu to protect herself from the villain, for the kung fu master had warned her that if she learned kung fu, she would be able to refuse the unwanted marriage, but that she would also scare other men from proposing to her. Pok To suddenly realizes that the woman he is talking to is in fact Wing Chun, and he forces her to admit the truth.

Obviously, Wing Chun's independence and fighting skills came with a high price in the sense that they put pressure on her female identity. The resolution of the narrative involves regaining that lost part of herself, and, as the one male person who is not threatened by Wing Chun's fighting skills, Pok To plays an important role in this process. This type of male character who steps aside while his female partner or wife engages in a duel with an adversary can be found in several of the Hong Kong martial arts classics such as *A Touch of Zen, The Temple of the Red Lotus,* or *The Deaf and Mute Heroine/Long e jian* (Wu Ma, 1971). On the level of narrative structuring the lost part of Wing Chun's self is retrieved through the rescue of Charmy. Wing Chun figures as a masculine version of herself, but it is precisely because Charmy figures as Wing Chun that the restructuring of Wing Chun's subjectivity can be realized.

History as Present

The examination of the process of telling where the fabula is mirrored in the film's story demonstrates that the structuring of (Wing Chun's) subjectivity is interdependent with the structuring of the narrative. Furthermore, by means of this process of telling, a new fabula and an improved subjectivity is produced. More precisely, the old fabula is mirrored in the new one through the doubling of Wing Chun in Charmy. By the same token (through this very doubling), an opportunity is created for the production of a new fabula, and hence, of a new "Wing Chun."

The use of history to tell/mark the present in the New Hong Kong Cinema that Ackbar Abbas discusses in his *Hong Kong: Culture and Politics of Disappearance* can also be observed as a need to (re)produce the ever-escaping Hong Kong subject (Abbas 1997). Concretely, in his discussion of the politics of the kung fu genre, Abbas asserts that the genre can be observed as an indirect representation of the changing nature of coloniality in Hong Kong. He points out that the ethos of mainly *male* heroism and personal prowess stands central to the genre (my emphasis). Generally, in the traditional swordplay and kung fu films, particularly the films of King Hu, Chang Che and Bruce Lee, fantasies of crushing the representatives of a corrupt system and/or defeating foreign invaders are played out, and an imaginary solution is repeatedly offered to the territorialized sense of self. In the case of Bruce Lee patriotism expresses itself as a form of anticolonialism, whereas with Jackie Chan the genre is transformed into kung fu comedy.[3] In Tsui Hark's case, Abbas is referring specifically to his *Wong Fei Hung* series (*Once Upon a Time in China*) where, as he states, colonialism is on the point of becoming obsolete. Finally, through Wong Kar-wai the heroes undergo a process of decomposition, as it were, which leads to the degeneration and self-destruction of the genre.

In respect to these assertions, elsewhere I have argued that although Hong Kong is a natural, historical, and social territory, the countering of its territorial regimes can be traced through cinematic images. This implies that the characters who soar, leap and speed through the mental territory, operate in such a way as to counter the regimes of the physical territory.[4] But it is even more pertinent for this study, that the territorial regimes countered through these actions are regimes of signs. As I stated earlier, these actions conditioned by the legal sensibility of the Chinese cultural imaginary, have a deterritorializing effect on the dominant structures of meaning, in particular those at work in the West. One fixation that these films definitely challenge is the Freudian division of the sexes between men as active and women as passive.[5] It is useful to recall that it was not until the 1990s that female characters started to appear on a more regular basis in Hollywood's action/adventure films, and even then, as I have noted in the previous section, the fictional worlds featuring some of the most famous women of action were set into the future.

In the case of kung fu comedy, and this is especially traceable in Yuen Woo Ping's body of work, authority figures are generally problematic whether they are Chinese or foreign invaders, corrupt or honest. As a kung fu comedy, *Wing Chun* can make fun of the incompetence, if not the absence, of (male/patriarchal/paternal) authority. The overt twisting of the principal rules of the martial arts tradition, which is celebrated for its dignified male heroes, gives way to the unprecedented emergence of empowering, albeit bizarre female characters. Surely, Yuen's films are not the only Hong Kong kung fu comedies from the early 1990s where a woman gives face to patriarchy; a very indicative example is the film *Fong Sai Yuk/ Fang Shi Yu* (Corey Yuen, 1994), where the main female character, who is a skilled kung fu fighter, allows her husband to beat her in public so as to "give him face." In addition, when her son, Fong Sai Yuk, loses a kung fu duel with a woman fighter, the mother enters the contest pretending to be Fong Sai Yuk's older brother in order to give face to the family name.[6]

Re-framing Imaginary Solutions

Even though in broader terms fabulation can be understood as telling or narrating I will use this term to refer to the re-construction of subjectivity, as it is dependent with the re-structuring of the narrative. This is the precondition for the emergence of new imaginary solutions, and/or the re-framing the old ones.[7] Through the re-framing of the fabula, a new imaginary solution is offered or, as is the case with *Wing Chun*, a new "Wing Chun" is produced. I have already introduced Deleuze and Guattari's notion of "creative fabulation" to underscore the possibility of countering territorial regimes of signs, and speaking of women of action, I have attributed this process to the Chinese cultural heritage. While the process of re-framing imaginary solutions cannot be defined in strictly Deleuze and Guattari's terms as creative fabulation, it is nevertheless closely related to the postmodern tendency to redefine myths, to give a new face to history or simply to "improve," in most cases, the male subject.

This tendency that certainly holds for new Hollywood cinema pertains to a great extent to Hong Kong cinema and as noted above, it is especially evident in the re-telling of the legends of Wong Fei Hung in Tsui Hark's *Once Upon a Time in China/Wong Fei Hung* series. In brief, in the course of the story telling process, the fabula is not only shaped and framed but it is revised, and ultimately, a new history (a new fabula) is produced.[8] Via this process a new subject can be produced and an old one can be "repaired" or "improved". In that sense, I am arguing that the process of re-framing imaginary solutions is linked with the re-framing of both the subjectivity and the fabula.

The re-framing of Wing Chun's subjectivity is bound up with "gender trouble" —she has to recover her femininity and prove to be the best fighter. When this is accomplished, her status as an authority on the side of good is confirmed. In that respect Wing Chun is an example of how female subjectivity in general can be re-framed. This potential, expressed on the level of the fictional world, is dependent on concerns and ideas that exceed this level. More precisely, "creative fabulation" is interconnected with a concrete cultural imaginary, and secondly, as is the case with Yuen Woo Ping's filmic universe, it is related to the idiosyncrasies of his persona as a filmmaker but also to the specificities of the cultural context. Therefore, the process of re-framing or re-vision always requires a higher narrational authority; in *Wing Chun* this authority in the first instance refers to the entity that brings meaning into the tension between the "old Wing Chun" and the "new" one, between her present masculinized self and her past feminine self. Wing Chun's teacher, Ng Mui can be understood as the personification of this narrational authority, which is evident on the level of the fabula and the level of filmic storytelling. In a specific sample scene that I analyze closely in Chapter 3, she gives Wing Chun a metaphorical lesson on how to defeat the chief bandit. Wing Chun manages to interpret the signs and employ the strategies that will enable her to win the final duel. This is crucial for setting the fictional world of this kung fu comedy into balance because her defeating the bandit Wing Chun proves that a woman can be the most capable fighter. Hence, the Buddhist nun who inspired Wing Chun to devise her own "female" fighting method plays the decisive role in the re-framing of Wing Chun's subjectivity. The remarkable aspect of this imaginary solution is that it is based on an alternative world view, a view that counters the territorial regimes of dominant patriarchal structures.

Creative Fabulations and Female Subjectivity

The laws of common sense play an important role when considering the socially and culturally imaginable story worlds, characters, and actions, and we often have the impression that these fabulations are putting pressure on more common sense notions of what is acceptable and logical in a feature film. The concern for fabulations and narrative structuring calls for a narrotological approach, whereas the concern for "creative fabulations" evokes ideas of art bound up with the deterritorialization of signs and countering dominant structures of meaning. For this reason I find Deleuze and Guattari's concepts to be a valuable complement to the narratological approach. This may perhaps seem like a contradictory combination because Deleuze and Guattari urge a deterritorialization of the sign and a flight from (dominant) structures of meaning, whereas critical narratology demands a close examination of the semiotics of storytelling with the purpose of locating and identifying these structures of meaning. Nevertheless, this seemingly contradictory process can prove productive for the type of endeavor in question. The point of departure is that Yuen Woo Ping's Hong Kong films can counter specific regimes of signs, that is, the structures of meaning dependent on cultural fixations, on the norms and rules that govern the Western imagination. Accordingly, these semiotic structures regulate the representation of femininity. It is thus logical that we need to be aware of the regimes of signs and the structures that give them shape, but we also have to consider the ways in which these films work to counter territorializing regimes and enable alternative universes to come "out of a shadow by a beam of light."

Just as pertinently, the recourse to Deleuze and Guattari's ideas is most useful in articulating the *art* inherent in kung fu comedies, such as those of Yuen Woo Ping that do not rely on complex characters or refined storylines but are instead invested in perfecting the action scenes. Considering that the process of "becoming-Wing Chun," is intertwined with narrative structuring, in terms of methodology the narratological approach is the logical choice. At this point we have to recall that one of the defining features of this filmic narrative is its crisis of female subjectivity and that setting the fictional world into balance will prove interdependent with "becoming Wing Chun," or rather, with re-figuring Wing Chun's subjectivity. In respect to these concerns, the choice of methodology does not immediately solve the problem, especially when taking into consideration that there is no existing theory of filmic narration that is subject-oriented. For this reason, I have developed my own method based on Bal's subject-oriented semiotic approach to narrative.[9]

In contrast to the view endorsed by cognitivist theories of filmic narration whereby subjectivity in cinema is discussed only in relation to the subjective use of the camera, my position is that subjectivity in cinema is not a unified investment.[10] Bal's theory of narrative corresponds to this view and the concept that I have taken as the point of departure is that of mapping subject positions according to their semiotic activities.[11] This approach presupposes that the subject is engaged in different forms of the meaning making process, or rather that it is implicated in diverse features of narrative semiosis. In terms of cinematic narration, the semantic network of the positions of represented subjects can be mapped for each scene, segment, or shot in such a way that the signs of subjectivity can be established on the basis of the relationships between subject positions. In a filmic narrative such as *Wing Chun,* represented subjects can principally be observed in terms of their function as diegetic agents, i.e., characters.

Determining the Network of Subjects

The character who has the capacity and the power to see, whose vision we share, has the advantage over other characters, and thus accordingly functions as the subject of vision. The character who has the capacity to act and to directly affect the course of events can be termed the subject of action; in *Wing Chun* the subject of action is most strikingly expressed through the main female character. Hence, by tracing the relationship between subject positions, we can establish the subjects of action, vision and narration; this implies that a particular scene, part of a scene, sequence, or even single shot can be understood as a unit of narrative discourse depending on the intersubjective engagement in question.

By tracing the relation between represented subjects, we can also establish the markers of the crisis of patriarchy in this film. A very indicative example is the relation between Wing Chun and her father. Wing Chun's father is a conservative man of tradition, but he has no power. It is rather Wing Chun who keeps up the pretense of his authority through filial behavior. While legendary female warriors are known to be filial,[12] the mocking of respectful behavior and subverting patriarchal authority is more typical of the kung fu comedies of the 1990s. Wing Chun acts like an obedient daughter around her father and she pleads with Aunt Fong not to aggravate him with stories of female independence. In other words, Wing Chun tries to "give him face." Similarly, Yuen Woo Ping's kung fu comedies that I discuss in Chapter 4 explicitly express the urgency of preserving the face of both patriarchy and paternity. Those who play the pivotal role in giving these fictional worlds "face" are female characters. Therefore, tracing the way subjectivity is structured and restructured, composed, or deconstructed provides the basis for understanding where and how, both meaning and cultural framings come into the filmic text. Most importantly, it enables us to trace the deterritorializing effects generated through the process of cinematic narration that I have described as the art of empowering female characters.

Female Authority Confirmed through the "Empowerment-Image"

In all the scenes where Wing Chun's authority is questioned and successfully confirmed, leading to the ultimate creation of the "universe of Mom" she relies on martial arts. As I have explained, the process of "becoming Wing Chun" is interdependent with narrative structuring, but we also need to consider this process as dependent upon, to put it in Deleuze's and Guattari's terms, the dynamics of speed and slowness, movement and rest occurring in the zone of microfemininity. Of significance is the fact that the fighting method she uses in the final duel is one of her own invention. The point of her new strategy, as transmitted metaphorically by her kung fu master, is that force need not be countered with force; a softer style can be even more effective. In an imaginative way, her new style, the "Wing Chun *kuen*" will coincide with the awakening of her hitherto subdued, feminine self. Her becoming a feminine version of herself is thus not connected to imitation, because her female identity is inextricable from her original, female fighting method.

Due to her consistent involvement in action (a characteristic backed up also by extratextual reference) Wing Chun's character-image can be associated with the cinema of the movement-image. Deleuze discusses three types of movement-images: perception-images (what is seen), affection-images (expression of feeling) and action-images (duration of action). For Deleuze, the movement-image belonged to the cinema of intensified narrative drive inherent in action cinema.[13] The movement-image can produce sense relations that, according to Deleuze, differ greatly from those of the time-image. In contrast, the time-image puts perception in contact with thought rather than action. Wing Chun's character-image certainly depends on the narrative drive of an action cinema, but the fact that it is a female character that can execute such spectacular, effective, and productive action articulated through the dynamic of speed and slowness creates a unique sense relation that I have described as the sense of empowerment. The specificity of the action that she is able to perform, and this is intrinsic to cinema, is the high level of kinematic energy, the exchange of speed and slowness that creates the sense of female empowerment.

By means of this sense relation, Wing Chun's character-image can figure as an empowerment-image. It infers a powerful female subject predicated on the connection between the screen and the cultural imaginary.

Conclusion

On the diegetic level, Wing Chun has the highest authority, and this is confirmed through her actions that repeatedly demonstrate that a woman *can* be a better pugilist than a man. Since we are dealing with the genre of kung fu comedy, the specific elaboration of issues related to power and gender produce a comical effect. The analyses of specific scenes in Chapter 3 will confirm that this is continually pronounced in the duels between Wing Chun and arrogant men. These are precisely the instances that generate the sense of empowerment and where Wing Chun's character-image can be perceived as an empowerment-image.

We can conclude that, apart from fabulation, the art of empowerment is closely bound up with the sense relation generated on the level of filmic images. This also implies that, in order to trace the re-definition of Wing Chun as a subject, which coincides with setting the fictional world into balance, we need to consider the process of cinematic storytelling. "Becoming Wing Chun" is interdependent with the action that generates the sense of empowerment and this action can be examined on the level of cinematic storytelling. To trace the strategies of cinematic storytelling that bring about the sense of empowerment, in Chapter 3 I observe the re-structuring of Wing Chun's subjectivity through the sequence of filmic scenes that feature Wing Chun as a fighter. I will bring to the fore the cinematic devices employed for the ultimate (re)construction of Wing Chun's subjectivity. We will find that, in order to trace the process of re-framing, it is necessary to establish a connection between the concerns expressed on the level of the fabula and the actual process of cinematic storytelling. It is through this process of re-presenting the film's fabula that the art of female empowerment is affirmed.

3

The Power of Female Action

Wing Chun: A "Flat" or a "Dense" Character?

Considering that Wing Chun's main function in this narrative is to propel action, she can also be understood as a frame of reference, a slot to be filled. The fact that she is elaborated as a "flat" rather than a "psychologically round" character may give the impression that this film is banal, too obvious, and overtly simplistic. In terms of cinematic storytelling, the construction of Wing Chun's character-image is basically restricted to a series of tableaux where she repeatedly overpowers her male opponents. According to David Bordwell, by American standards many Hong Kong films (of all genres) "look broadly played, perhaps seeming closer to silent film conventions than to those post-Method Hollywood." Bordwell suggests that this is part of a distinct aesthetic in which expressive amplification is central to the performance of actor and ensemble (Bordwell 2000: 88).

When it comes to the traditional notions of cinematic art, style in principle refers to the systematic or inventive use of cinematic devices as these are related to the process of narration, and therefore, "broadness" presumes in fact a certain simplicity of expression.[1] It has been pointed out that by the standards of festival cinema the Hong Kong approach to narrative seems obstinately naïve. Film scholars suggest, however, that in place of overarching coherence, we should look for a tension between "spectacle" and "narrative" (Bordwell 2000: 178). In keeping with the themes and methods of this study, I am referring to the "art" in *Wing Chun* in the vein of Deleuze and Guattari, hence as an art of countering territorial regimes, or more precisely, the art of empowering female characters. This presupposes in the first place an emphasis on the narrative representation of issues such as gender and power.

In *Wing Chun* the women are principally on the side of good, whereas the men (with the exception of Pok To) are bad (and potential oppressors), weak, or ridiculous. Wing Chun can thus primarily be defined in terms of her position within the fabula because on the level of the story her principal aims as an actor are not developed further so as to display complexity and psychological depth. I am referring to the notion of "actor" in the narratological sense, as operating on the level of the fabula, and hence, before it is developed into a character through the storytelling process.

Discussing Wing Chun's "flatness" within the narratological framework then, I would add that her status as a character overlaps with her position as an actor. According to A. J. Greimas, an actor is a structural position, while a character is a complex semantic unit. Bal adds that the character is the actor provided with distinctive characteristics, which together create the effect of a character. On the basis of semantic content, that is, of different principles that work together, the image of the character is constructed.

The actors have an intention: they aspire toward an aim. That aspiration is the achievement of something agreeable or favorable, or the evasion of something disagreeable or unfavorable [...] An actant is a class of actors that shares a certain characteristic quality. That shared characteristic is related to the teleology of the fabula as a whole. An actant is therefore a class of actors whose members have an identical relation to the aspect of telos which constitutes the principle of the fabula. (Bal 1997: 197)

Here, we also have to consider the fact that kung fu comedy as a genre makes much less of an appeal to authenticity, reminding us also that kung fu comedy draws its origins from Beijing opera. A. C. Scott observed that the Chinese "have always sought their enjoyment in theater in the sensory immediacy of the actor's presentation"[2] (A. C. Scott 1983: 160). Moreover, the movie plays with certain types, such as those of the comic actors, the *chou,* but more pertinently, Wing Chun's character-image echoes the female type skilled in fighting and riding and accustomed to forceful action. This type of character provided ample opportunities for spectacular displays of acrobatics and different combat forms but it retained at the same time its feminine appeal.[3] The point is that Wing Chun's simplicity and "flatness" is additionally purported by the concrete expectations based on extratextual information inherent in this cultural stereotype. While it draws its origins in tradition however, one of the main intentions of kung fu comedy is to simultaneously subvert tradition and mock the principals of the martial arts genre. "Gender trouble" is an example of such subversion and so is the mocking of filial piety. This is acceptable precisely because there is less appeal to authenticity.

Taking into account Wing Chun's function in the fabula, I would argue that her "flatness," transparency, and simplicity secures her "density" and stability as a female heroine; paradoxically perhaps, her ability to act as the protector on the side of good and execute a series of effective physical performances which cause that "flatness," generates at the same time a sense of empowerment. The sense of empowerment conditions and confirms ultimately her image as a female warrior.

Re-framing Female Subjectivity through Action

The main objective in the narrative is to free the village of the bandits and at the same time solve the tension between masculine and feminine forces. In the analysis that follows this tension will be examined in relation to Wing Chun's capacity to act as a fighter. Consequently, the analysis of pertinent sample scenes will show that fabulation as a precondition for the re-framing of Wing Chun's subjectivity is interdependent with the process of cinematic storytelling. Therefore, when discussing Wing Chun's subjectivity in filmic terms, apart from taking into account the elements of narrative (the level of the fabula) and the aspects of narrative (the level of the story), it is necessary to consider the signifiers that are specifically cinematic. I am referring, for example, to framing, duration, angle, shot/reverse shot, camera movement, or editing. An examination of the connection between cinematic signifiers and the structuring of the narrative reveals what kind of character-images and, implicitly, subjects are generated via filmic narratives. More importantly, it provides additional insight into the ways a seemingly "flat" character such as Wing Chun can nevertheless create a sense of empowerment on the level of the filmic images.

The analyses of concrete scenes will demonstrate that, as a character, Wing Chun functions primarily as the subject of action, that is, she represents and personifies the subject of action. She has to protect the people from the bandits or defend the female honor, hence she *takes* action and she is continuously *engaged* in physical action. Since the process of structuring whereby Wing

Chun's subjectivity is re-framed evolves sequentially and can be examined on the basis of her character-image, I have made a selection of pertinent scenes as they are related to the fabula.

The Dynamics of Keeping Still (Sample Scene 1)

The bandits seem to be an everyday threat, and Wing Chun is the only one who can fight them off effectively. On the basis of their first encounter, we can easily conclude that these men are no match for Wing Chun. She is outnumbered, but she can defeat them while seated and using the scholar Wong (Waise Lee) as a buffer-puppet. I have selected a series of shots that include the scholar Wong's verbal clash with the bandits, their attack, Wing Chun's intervention and her successful resolution of the problem. In the opening of the scene there is an exchange of shots between Wong and the bandits. Wong is standing in front of a window of a hut, and we notice Wing Chun seated behind the scholar inside the hut. The bandits appear ready to jump him from right and left. Suddenly a stool flies out of the hut, hits one of the bandits while Wong ducks. Wing Chun somersaults out of the hut and lands elegantly on the ground, perfectly keeping her balance. In the following shot, she sits on the stool and crosses her leg in a manly fashion, rests one hand on her left knee and the other on her right thigh. She looks like she is ready to observe the fight rather than be involved in it.

In the wide shot in which Wing Chun launches herself out of the window, the frame is canted, implying that the horizon is at a diagonal angle (Still 3.1). The canted frame recurs in subsequent shots, where Wing Chun assumes her position on the stool (Still 3.2). Considering that Wing Chun is seated, the canted frame alludes to a certain dynamic that at first does not correspond to the stillness of the body. Due to the canted frame, Wing Chun marks the diagonal line of the image; this is especially pronounced in the medium close-ups of Wing Chun (Still 3.3).

Still 3.1

Still 3.2

Still 3.3

Stills 3.1, 3.2, 3.3 Like the one-armed White Nun from Louis Cha's martial arts novel *The Deer and the Cauldron*, Wing Chun can also fight while seated.

Therefore, the pertinent filmic signifier in this segment is framing, more precisely the level of the shots. For those who are more familiar with Hong Kong martial arts films, the canted frame is not new; this device is used regularly in scenes depicting fights; the combatants (the hero in particular) are frequently depicted in this manner. The fact that Yuen Woo Ping uses this device to frame a character that is seated tells us something about the specific dynamic related to this character. We soon realize that Wing Chun is not moving, and yet she can generate action. This is confirmed in the shot where she uses a stick to "operate" Wong's body (Still 3.4). With her stick she sets Wong into a forward motion, hence he falls on the bandits, and when the bandits push him back, Wing Chun employs the same strategy (Still 3.5).

Still 3.4   Still 3.5

Stills 3.4, 3.5 A very indicative distribution of power — Wing Chun as the puppeteer and scholar Wong as the buffer-puppet.

At this point it is necessary to note the importance Yuen Woo Ping places on perfecting the action scenes and making the fights both attractive and convincing. His training in Beijing opera can be traced through his affinities as film director and action choreographer; the first and the most important aspect of this influence is his investment in refining the choreography of the movements rather than insisting on new drafts of the script. Taking into consideration the performers in Yuen's films we could say that his art of countering territorial regimes through action rests to a great extent on teaming up with actors who are accomplished martial arts experts. Jackie Chan's big debut, *Snake in the Eagle's Shadow/She xing diao shou/Se ying diu sau,* was also Yuen's first feature as a director. Chan was a Beijing opera trainee and just as actor/director/action choreographer Sammo Hung, director Corey Yuen, kung fu cult hero Yuen Biao and acrobat-turned-actor Yuen Wah, he was a student at Master Yu Jim Yuen's Chinese opera school and one of the Seven Little Fortunes, a boys' performance troupe. Apart from Jackie Chan, as already mentioned, Yuen Woo Ping also engaged his father Simon Yuen Siu Tien, an experienced actor and one of Hong Kong cinema's first generation of martial-arts directors to star in his first three features, *Snake in the Eagle's Shadow*, *Drunken Master,* and *Dance of the Drunk Mantis.*[4]

In Yuen Woo Ping's film the *Magnificent Butcher/Lin shi rong* (1979), Sammo Hung appears in the leading role, and in the film *Dreadnaught* Yuen Biao, a well-known martial artist and another one of the Seven Little Fortunes, plays the coward. Donnie Yen, who plays the lead in *Drunken Tai Chi*, was trained in the martial arts from the age of four by his mother. In one of his interviews he states that in this film the time and energy were devoted to one aspect of the film — the physical performance of the actors.[5] In *The Tai Chi Master,* Yuen Woo Ping worked with Jet Li, the Chinese national champion in the sport of wu shu, a performance martial art combining elements of traditional kung fu, gymnastics and Chinese opera.[6] Yuen's concern with perfecting the action cannot be overstated because martial arts performances and action govern not only the structure of the narrative, but also the working of the *mise-en-scène*, the camera work, and the editing, as well as the formal interventions within the filmic image (such as the framing, for example).

The fact that Yuen places strong emphasis on perfecting the choreographed movements implies that he does not rely on editing techniques as a primary tool to depict/"tell" the action. What this means in the case of the concrete scene from *Wing Chun* is that three out of four accounts of Wong being pushed by Wing Chun (losing balance and knocking out the bandits) are elaborated in one shot. In this kung fu comedy, the action elaborated in one shot gives the scene a slapstick-like quality. The one who emerges as a clown is the scholar Wong (but also the equally incompetent intruders), while Wing Chun maintains a dignified appearance throughout the entire scene. Taking into account her performance in this sample scene, Wing Chun needs to be observed as a spectacle and as an agent whose function is to propel action.

Moreover, she is depicted as the "puppeteer," the one who controls the event; it is thus thanks to her skills that the mockery is staged. Once the fight is over, the frame regains a sense of gravity.

A female fighter engaged in combat without leaving her chair is an empowerment-image that draws its roots from the past and from other media; in the martial arts novel *The Deer and the Cauldron/ Lu ding ji,* by Louis Cha/Jin Yong, one of the most superior and authoritative female characters, the one-armed White Nun, just as Wing Chun, is capable of fighting fiercely while seated.

Wing Chun: The Defender of the People (Sample Scene 2)

At the beach festival, Wing Chun is again the one who has to fight off the intruders. The village officials know they are all safe as long as she is present. Nevertheless, when Wing Chun steps forward to take action, a group of local men complain to her father that she should step back rather than try to overshadow them. As expected, the bandits beat up these pompous men and Wing Chun has to take charge. Again, she easily manages to defeat a horde of men on her own.

The pertinent cinematic signifier in this scene is camera movement; in fight 1, Wing Chun punches one opponent. The camera follows her movement to the left as she delivers a heavy push in the chest to another one. In the same shot, Wing Chun turns swiftly to the right to fend off the previous adversary and then she turns to the left to kick the other one. The camera pans again to follow her movement. The fighting continues as she kicks the intruder on the right, and then she gives an additional kick to a third opponent that pops up into the shot from the right. The shot ends as Wing Chun blocks a blow from the first opponent on this side.

The same strategy will be employed in fight 3, where the camera pans left and right as Wing Chun in medium shot fights two opponents, now using a sword. In fight 2 she is shown performing acrobatic movements, flying up and through the air, fighting several opponents simultaneously. A series of moves depicted in one single shot makes the duel more convincing and enhances the impression that Wing Chun is an extremely skilled fighter. She does more than defeat the bandits: she ultimately mocks their fighting techniques. Wing Chun whacks one of them on the head with a sword and gives the other a thump on the arm, causing him to drop his weapon.

Considering that the series of moves and blows are depicted in single shots, it is not difficult to conclude that an actress who was trained in martial arts was required for this role, hence a person who possesses such skills (at least to a certain level). Apart from Yuen Woo Ping's genius as an action choreographer, this kind of performance requires serious practice. Understandably, as is the case with other stars in Yuen's films, Yeoh's capacity to perform most of her stunt work contributes to the empowering features of Wing Chun's character-image.

Defending Female Honor (Sample Scene 3)

While the duel at the festival serves as a concrete purpose and results in the (first) rescue of Charmy (Catherine Hung Yan), the next fight is a set-piece; Wing Chun accepts the challenge of a local man who has come to "teach her a lesson." This fight does not propel action, but just as the first fight where scholar Wong is used as a buffer-puppet, it offers an empowering image of femininity. Already in the festival scene it was evident that not all men can accept the fact that a woman is the best fighter in the village, and this is confirmed once again as Wing Chun not only has to protect the village from the (male) intruders, but she also has to engage in duels with local bullies. Once more, Wing Chun wins the fight on her own terms and demonstrates that the misogynist contender is a laughable person. As in sample scene 1, where she controls the situation while seated on a stool, in this scene too, Wing Chun defeats her opponent with a minimum of effort; again, her superior fighting technique enables her not only to defeat the male opponent but also to make a fool of him. For a start, the pathetic contender uses both hands to attack Wing Chun, while she fights with only one hand.

The fight takes place in Wing Chun's dining room, a domestic, womanly space that also needs to be defended, it seems. During the fight, Wing Chun plays with a tray filled with tofu, a soft, creamy substance that would be so easy to crush if her rival could only get close enough. Wing Chun keeps inviting him to take the tofu from the tray but each time he approaches the tray he suffers a series of kicks, punches and blows. The harder he tries to seize the tofu the sillier he appears; the tray even shoots up in the air, spins and circles around the room while the pigheaded man is hit with extra force (Still 3.6). Just as he cannot strike a decent blow that would prove that a man is a better pugilist than a woman, he cannot smash Wing Chun's tofu.

Still 3.6 Again, Wing Chun defeats her male opponent with a minimum of effort.

Female Inter-Action (Sample Scene 4)

Defending female honor and female independence is quite important, because the three women have no one to depend on except themselves. Instead of female action, this scene in the center of the narrative is about female inter-action. We need to recall that already in the beginning of the film a self-sufficient female household is introduced — self-sufficient because Aunt Fong is the entrepreneur and Wing Chun is the protector and also mistaken for "the man/master of the house." Aunt Fong or Abacus Fong (Yuen King Tan) runs the soya bean curd business and generally her main interest in life is financial profit. She is independent and rational and lacks typically female traits such as kindheartedness, sensitivity, or compassion. It is not surprising then that she turns out to be the perfect match for the devious and opportunistic scholar Wong. He tries to win Wing Chun's hand in marriage (so she could protect his property), but at the same time he lusts for Charmy. In the end, Abacus Fong tricks the rich scholar into her bed and into marrying her. She is vocal, and unlike Wing Chun who (literally) lets her actions speak, Abacus yells and screams and every once in a while blurts out feminist statements. She warns Wing Chun's younger sister, who is newly married, not to lose "their (female) face"; she thereby also subverts the traditionalist/masculinist implications of "losing (the) face" (of patriarchy).

Charmy joins the female household after her husband's death, when Wing Chun and Abacus Fong (with the scholar Wong's money) bid the highest price for her. In contrast to Wing Chun and her aunt, Charmy represents that vulnerable side of femininity that needs protection. The multiple sides of femininity can best be observed in the scene where the three women soak their feet and talk about their differences. Charmy sees marriage as the best possible option for herself since she is neither a heroine like Wing Chun nor a business woman like Fong. She thinks she has two opportunities for marriage, but in fact Wing Chun and her aunt will marry the men she is counting on. The inter-action between the women sharpens our awareness of the multiple versions of femininity and it brings forth the idea of female self-reliance. Charmy, unlike Wing Chun, flaunts her sexuality, and in this scene of female bonding she quite directly (by means of foot massage) offers bodily pleasure to her companions. Charmy knows exactly which erogenous zone on the female foot needs to be pressed to trigger sexual enjoyment. A detail of a foot (the sexual fetish *par excellence*) is depicted being massaged by two hands, and in shots that follow (Abacus), and (Wing Chun), the women are screaming giddily, evidently discovering the erotic side of foot massage (Stills 3.7–3.9).

Still 3.7

Still 3.8

Still 3.9

Stills 3.7–3.9 Female inter-action that plays with the idea of female self-sufficiency.

Therefore, in spite of the fact that it brings up the female discourse of heterosexual love and marriage, this female inter-action at the same time plays with the idea of female self-sufficiency.

Sparring with the Fortress Master, Faced with a Crisis (Sample Scene 5)

In a world where male weakness and inefficiency is so overt, it is not strange that the idea of female self-sufficiency would emerge.

In this kung fu comedy, problematic masculinity is taken to yet another level, however; while in the hitherto encounters with male fighters Wing Chun's superiority may have had a castrating effect in the symbolic sense, in the scene with the Flying Monkey (Norman Chu), the abductor of Charmy, the act of castration is literal. When chasing after this bandit, Wing Chun throws a burning spear that flies directly into his private parts. In one of the subsequent scenes, he comments on his inability to perform as a man.

The chief of the bandits, Flying Monkey, takes this incident as an occasion to visit Wing Chun and create an opportunity for his subordinate to kidnap Charmy. In fact, he organizes the kidnapping of Charmy in order to lure Wing Chun to his fortress. The spar with Flying Monkey is the longest and the most elaborate one in the film, and he is the first and only opponent who cannot be easily eliminated. In that sense, the duration of the scene and the number of shots can be taken as a pertinent filmic signifier; the scene consists of approximately 120 shots that principally depict Wing Chun in a defensive guard, re-acting to Flying Monkey, devising ways to block his advances. In the previous fights she was able to defeat her opponents with minimum effort, but in this case she has to be extra vigilant. A large portion of the duel is elaborated in shots that depict a series of strikes and punches that needed to be rehearsed and choreographed. As Michelle Yeoh, Norman Chu[7] who plays Flying Monkey, is able to execute the complicated and demanding stunt work. Neither one of them needs a stunt double.

Flying Monkey determines the rhythm and pace of the fight: he decides when to pause and indulge in self-praise, when to pose an offensive question, and when to make a sexist comment. He asks Wing Chun if she is married and adds immediately that it would be difficult for an ordinary man to control her. Flying Monkey also attempts to kiss her and as expected, provokes a furious reaction. On top of this, he uses the "cotton belly" technique, that is, he has the ability to absorb his opponent's fist (and thereby the blow itself) with his belly.

The verbal sparring is elaborated in the classical style of the shot/reverse shot method. The segment in which Flying Monkey proposes a kiss starts with a close-up of Wing Chun, followed by a close-up of Flying Monkey, but when the physical power struggle resumes they are together in the shot, in a medium-close up with the wooden practicing dummy between them. Flying Monkey tries to seize Wing Chun's hand, but she resists. If we consider Flying Monkey's capacity to take the initiative and remain one step ahead in the duel, his claim that he is the only man who can control Wing Chun does not seem so preposterous after all. This, of course, is the cause of the major crisis in this narrative that needs urgently to be solved.

Wing Chun and Flying Monkey's Phallic Weapon (Sample Scene 6)

In this type of world, Wing Chun constantly has to deal with men who either want to confirm their masculinity by challenging her martial arts skills, or, as the morally corrupt scholar Wong tries to do, appropriate her skills for their own personal benefit. There would be nothing wrong if a man wanted to employ her for a salary, but Wong's initial idea is to marry her because that way he would not have to pay for her services. Wong cannot outsmart her, however. Already in the very beginning of the film Wing Chun uses him as a buffer-puppet to ward off the bandits. Their chief, the Flying Chimpanzee, is determined to prove that he is the only one who can control Wing Chun. In spite of his regressive fixation, the chief bandit is the only opponent who is not immediately overpowered by Wing Chun, but instead urges her serious engagement and attention. The only man who does not feel threatened by Wing Chun's fighting skills/authority is her childhood sweetheart Pok To. He doesn't have a problem with the fact that his fighting techniques are inferior, and therefore, he is the only man who can play a productive role in the restitution of her femininity.

The first duel with Chimpanzee at the bandits' fortress follows Wing Chun's renewed romance with Pok To. He accompanies Wing Chun to the fortress to assist her, but he is eliminated at the very outset. Wing Chun has no one to rely on except herself. As in the past/the legend, the stakes of the duel are high — if Wing Chun wins, Charmy will be freed, and if she loses, she will become Flying Monkey's wife. History is repeating itself, but on this occasion a double rescue takes place as she rescues her friend Charmy, and for the second time in her life, she saves herself from an unwanted marriage.

This is not a simple endeavor, however. As stated earlier, the chief of the bandits is especially fixated on proving that he is the only man who can control Wing Chun. As in the previous duel, he is offensive and makes sexual advances. In the middle of the brawl he manages to caress Wing Chun's cheek, and when she punches him in the face, he touches his cheek, smiling happily as if he has just been kissed. Once again, it seems, Wing Chun is forced to react to Flying Monkey's insolent behavior rather than to act on her own terms.

In spite of the fact that he is introduced as the best male fighter, his "manliness" is subverted by means of narration. More precisely, the spear he uses in the duel is supposedly so heavy that it needs to be carried by a group of his subordinates, implying of course that no ordinary man could lift it on his own. Nevertheless, the filmic signifiers undermine this display of manliness by over emphasizing the enormity of the weapon. This is especially evident in the shot where Flying Monkey is positioned in a canted frame, the spear pointed diagonally to the upper right corner of the image. The wide-angle lens expands the size of the spear and distorts its shape, turning it into a seemingly potent phallic object (Still 3.10).

Still 3.10 In the comical battle of the sexes Wing Chun has to prove that she can control her opponent's "manly" weapon.

The crucial task Wing Chun needs to accomplish in this comical battle of the sexes is to prove that she can control the "manly" weapon; she has to pull the spear out of a wall in three moves. Thanks to Flying Monkey, who accidentally pushes the spear through the wall, Wing Chun gains advantage in the duel; she flies over the wall, catches the spear and leaves Flying Monkey without his manly instrument (Stills 3.11–3.13).

Still 3.11

Still 3.12

Still 3.13

Stills 3.11–3.13 While Chimpanzee is ridiculed by means of filmic signifiers, Wing Chun's skills are elaborated as impressive.

She does not indulge in this act of symbolic castration, but tosses the spear back to its owner. If we compare the shot of Flying Monkey approaching the camera holding the spear, and the shot of Wing Chun holding the same weapon in the end of the scene, we can conclude that Flying Monkey is ridiculed by means of the filmic signifiers. Wing Chun is filmed in a semi-wide shot with a normal lens, and from this perspective, Flying Monkey's weapon looks surprisingly ordinary. What is impressive is the ease with which Wing Chun handles it.

Taking into account the ways in which the filmic signifiers affect the character-images of Wing Chun and Flying Monkey, we could say that the narrator is on the side of Wing Chun. In sample scenes 1 and 3, Wing Chun's contenders are mocked through their inferior fighting skills; in narratological terms, these actions are determined on the level of the fabula. In the case of Flying Monkey, Wing Chun still has to demonstrate her superiority as a fighter; in fact, she still has to devise a way to defeat him. In that sense, the fabula, just as the "new Wing Chun," still needs to be created. At the moment, Flying Monkey still believes he can defeat Wing Chun, and he challenges her to fight with him again in three days. Wing Chun is at pains to find a tactic she should use to defy Flying Monkey's "cotton belly" and finally affirm her superiority. The filmic signifiers in this sample scene "tell us" that, in spite of his exceptional fighting skills, winning a duel against the show-off chief bandit will not be an impossible feat.

Wing Chun's Teacher as the Personification of the Highest Narrational Authority (Sample Scene 7)

On the basis of the hitherto analyses of Wing Chun's character-image (on the level of action), we can conclude that she personifies the highest authority in her community. Various men call her authority into question, but without effect. The only one who causes a disruption within the power structure is the chief bandit, Flying Monkey. As it turns out, Wing Chun's main problem is not only how to win the final duel with Flying Monkey but how to turn *his* power and authority to *her* advantage. We will find that figuring the way to do the former will condition the accomplishment of the latter. With the help of her teacher, the Buddhist nun (Cheng Pei Pei), Wing Chun will realize that one need not necessarily use force to defy force. The ultimate lesson she will learn is that a woman need not give up her femininity to defeat a male fighter.

After the first fight at the bandits' fortress, Wing Chun goes to visit her master to consult with her. Thus far, we have established that, as a subject of action, Wing Chun personifies the highest authority and, furthermore, that the implied narrational authority, the subject of vision, is on her side. In this sample scene we witness Ng Mui's extraordinary teaching skills and authority as a martial arts master. Wing Chun looks up to her and is certainly influenced by her. This scene is another example of female inter-action and just as sample scene 4, it is elaborated in great contrast to the action-packed sample scenes. The teacher is seated on the bench in an elevated position in relation to Wing Chun, who is kneeling down on the ground in front of her. We first see the back of Ng Mui's head filmed from a higher angle. On the one hand, her higher status is immediately marked through Wing Chun's kneeling position, but on the other hand, by means of the high angle, they both seem subordinated to a "higher vision from above." In the following shot the teacher is filmed from a slightly lower angle, which confirms her higher status in the relationship.[8]

The teacher begins her lesson by biting into a nutshell and breaking a tooth. She then sweeps up a few dozen walnuts into the sleeve of her robe, flicks the sleeve a few times and smashes its contents against the tree trunk. When she unfolds the sleeve we see that the nuts have done all the work themselves, so to speak;

broken shells spill out and the pile of walnuts remains in the teacher's hand. The dynamic of this action is produced in one shot through a shift from the normal level of the frame to a canted view, as Ng Mui flicks her sleeve and then makes an upward motion (Stills 3.14, 3.15).

Still 3.14   Still 3.15

Stills 3.14, 3.15 Wing Chun's teacher Ng Mui, a Buddhist nun, provides a metaphoric answer to how one's strength can be used in the most productive way.

The following shot is a jump cut, the frame is not canted and we have the impression that Ng Mui is about to smash her sleeve against a different tree (Still 3.16).

Still 3.16 Ng Mui is about to smash a different tree.

Shots that follow are filmed from an extremely low angle creating yet another defamiliarizing effect. After that, the frame is canted again, the sleeve unfolds and the broken shells fall to the ground (Stills 3.17–3.19).

Still 3.17

Still 3.18

Still 3.19

Still 3.20

Still 3.21

Stills 3.17–3.21 Wing Chun's teacher is played by the icon of Hong Kong cinema, the legendary woman of action from the 1960s, Cheng Pei Pei.

The distorted level of the frame and the peculiar angle create a defamiliarizing effect, making this entire action appear simple, yet remarkable at the same time. This action is Ng Mui's metaphoric answer to Wing Chun's question of how to defeat Flying Monkey (Stills 3.20, 3.21). Similarly, her warning that Wing Chun will hurt herself if she tries to fight against a strong power, also needs to be understood in the metaphoric sense. Wing Chun will fully grasp the lesson about the productive use of force in a later scene, when she sees Pok To's futile effort to punch a mosquito. At the end of their meeting, the teacher tells Wing Chun that, no matter how strong she is, she should settle down and get married. Interestingly, this patriarchal piece of advice, as it were, is coming from the very woman who taught Wing Chun to protect herself from male dominance and oppression. In fact, the resolution of Wing Chun's duel with Chimpanzee is very much related to her ability to fight like a woman, to use the Wing Chun *kuen*. In terms of restoring her femininity, this could also mean that Wing Chun needs to harness her kung fu moves from her "weak" female side.

The implied paradox undermines the typically Freudian division between men as active and women as passive, implying also that, if a woman is to be active, she must be masculinized. As noted earlier, the masculinization of women in Hollywood films in the late 1980s and early 1990s as bound up with body politics and the *musculinization* of the female body, does not hold in this socio-cultural imaginary. What is more, in these fabulas the Freudian division between the sexes — active/men vs. passive/women — does not quite hold. Just as importantly, in Hong Kong cinema the women of action are not a phenomenon of the "future" conditioned by the feminist movement, as has often been the case with the action women in the West. In terms of Yuen Woo Ping's film, this is even confirmed through extratextual information; the role of Wing Chun's teacher is played by the icon of Hong Kong cinema, the legendary woman of action from the 1960s, Cheng Pei Pei, perhaps best known for her role in King Hu's classic, *Come Drink with Me* and more recently for her role as the notorious Jade Fox in *Crouching Tiger, Hidden Dragon.*

Since the Buddhist nun Ng Mui is the one who ultimately brings meaning to the play between strength and weakness, masculine and feminine, she can be understood as the personification of the highest narrational authority in *Wing Chun.*

In the Zone of Microfemininity: Becoming Wing Chun (Sample Scene 8)

Still 3.22

Still 3.23

Still 3.24

Still 3.25

Stills 3.22–3.25 Wing Chun's femininity is ultimately restored not just through her womanly appearance but through her fighting technique, that is, through her capacity to act.

In the final duel, the chief of the bandits uses another heavy spear hauled by a group of his helpers. In contrast, Wing Chun chooses the twin short swords comparable to the short weapons Cheng Pei

Pei uses in the film *Come Drink With Me* (Stills 3.22–3.25). Flying Monkey comments on her courage to use "such a short weapon against his champion spear." Wing Chun is quick to respond to his remark, but this only provokes new misogynist allusions.

At the very beginning of the encounter, Wing Chun lures Flying Monkey into a small room in a nearby cottage, and we soon discover the reason behind this tactic. Flying Monkey's spear is simply too big for this interior space, and predictably, its size prevents each move he attempts to make. A few times the spear even gets stuck between the ceiling and a wall, and Flying Monkey cannot do much to block Wing Chun's strikes. Her two short and sharp weapons prove effective indeed, as she briskly produces several cuts on Flying Monkey's body. Thanks to her clever strategy Wing Chun manages to completely turn Flying Monkey's strength *against* him; by the end of the cottage-episode he is wounded, disarmed, and startled by her sudden dominance as a fighter.

The duel continues in the exterior space, and one more time Wing Chun applies the new tactic. This time, she twists Flying Monkey's left arm, "disarming" him quite literally; then she strikes sharply at his right arm divesting it of its strength. With a swift push, she directs this now wobbly arm toward Flying Monkey's chest, the result of which is that he punches himself with such force that he is thrown on the ground. The duel continues in a similar fashion, but no matter how hard he is hit, Flying Monkey remains persistent until he finally collapses.

It is important to note that for her ultimate triumph Wing Chun is dressed as a woman. Throughout the entire film she wears a male costume, and we are able to get only a glimpse of how she looked in her "female days" through the doubling of Wing Chun's "Miss Soya Bean" image in Charmy. Apart from embracing her feminine self, in sample scene 8 she devises a new style of fighting; clearly she re-invents both her self and her fighting method. Speaking of Wing Chun's actions, then, on the level of the fabula they serve to bring law and order to the village. On the level of the story, through her actions she creates a sense of empowerment; though a woman, she confirms her role as the best fighter. Finally, as the best fighter, she also confirms her identity as a powerful female subject. The remarkable aspect of this filmic narrative is that Wing Chun's femininity is restored through her fighting technique, and hence through her capacity to act. Even though she has found her long lost love, Pok To, and has decided to marry him, it is not just by looking like a woman that the process of becoming "Wing Chun" is achieved — it is through the specific dynamics of movement and rest in the zone of microfemininity that her femaleness is retrieved.

Conclusion

As all the Chinese women warriors, Wing Chun belongs to a time far removed from our own; she is both a historical and a legendary figure, and she is part of a world where the only authority that has a higher status is her female teacher. Clearly, the symbolic universe where the Law of the Father is at work does not hold for *Wing Chun*. In fact, by winning the duel with Chimpanzee, she earns the right to be called "Mom." As the "Mom," she immediately orders the bandits to be "good." Considering Wing Chun's status in the narrative, we can conclude that *Wing Chun* is a rare example of a filmic text that functions according to the Law of the Woman, and that ultimately, it offers a painfully simplistic, yet incredibly empowering (albeit imaginary) solution to the crisis of femininity.

The balance of this fictional world is achieved across three levels, each of which is closely dependent on the working of female subjectivity: 1) female action, 2) female interaction, and 3) female personification of the highest narratorial authority. The restructuring of subjectivity is closely tied with the re-shaping of the fabula, whereby a history/legend about a woman warrior becomes intertwined with contemporary concerns with female empowerment. The fixing of the problem on the level of the fictional world coincides with the re-definition of female subjectivity.

The fact that in *Wing Chun* female subjectivity plays a defining function, that Wing Chun is a woman who can restore balance to the fictional world, a world where the only character who has a higher authority is her teacher, a Buddhist nun, is in the first instance dependent on (creative) fabulation. In respect to this, Yuen's filmic universe that I will discuss further in the next chapter is closely bound up with the legal sensibility of the concrete socio-cultural imaginary, but also with the subversion of its norms, rules, and laws. The creative aspect of this fabulation contingent on a specific legal sensibility is that it conditions the process of "becoming Wing Chun." Fabulation, which is interdependent with the process of cinematic storytelling, generates the sense of female empowerment.

The terms of the analysis introduced in this chapter will hold true for other filmic narratives. We will look at the relation between female empowerment expressed on the level of the storytelling process and the concerns conveyed on the level of the fabula. When it comes to Yuen Woo Ping's body of work, we will find that women of action, as a recurring motif in his kung fu comedies, repeatedly demonstrate that the traditional martial arts hero does not suffice in this filmic universe.

4

The Universe of Yuen Woo Ping

Creating New, Unexpected Connections and Blocks of Coexistence

Due to the specific aspects and elements of narrative bound up with cultural norms and rules, as well as filmic devices developed to cater these story worlds, Hong Kong films resist the approaches of more traditional film theory. As I suggested at the outset, one of the most important reasons why the Hong Kong martial arts genre is so appealing to international (predominantly Western) audiences is because these films frequently work contrary to the laws of common sense that govern the social imagination of Western traditions.

On the basis of a close analysis of the film *Wing Chun*, in the previous chapter I argued that Yuen Woo Ping's filmic universe can be observed as an art of empowering women, on both the level of the fabula (the macro unit) and the level of filmic scenes (the micro unit). I focused on the process of "becoming-woman," more precisely, of "becoming-Wing Chun." In this chapter, the analyses will show that the art of empowering female characters is intertwined with a series of "becomings" that occur in Yuen's films; these becomings, or blocks of coexistence as Deleuze and Guattari also call them, have a deterritorializing effect typical of Hong Kong cinema. In Yuen's films that I will discuss here, these include for instance, "becoming-mantis," "becoming-tai chi master," "becoming-Miss Ho" or "becoming a body without organs," evoking also Deleuze and Guattari's ultimate "becoming-BwO." As I will explain shortly, in cases where one of the main characters is a eunuch, becoming a BwO is quite literal, as in Yuen's film *The Tai Chi Master*.

What is common to the characters in these films is that they can be seen as superhuman or subhuman creatures, and they can even become animal-like. We should recall that specific punches and stances are derived from different animals, so a kung fu film may show the hero discovering a technique by observing an animal's attack. For example, in Yuen's *Snake in the Eagle's Shadow*, Jackie Chan imitates the movements of a snake inspired by a cobra's attack on a cat.[1] Even though such characters are not strictly animals, in certain moments they can act as gravity-defying creatures, and what is more, they can transform into a "white crane," or a "mantis," use a "tiger's claw" or a "snake's fang."

The discussion on becomings as related with Deleuzian aesthetics is relevant for the study at stake because the art of countering territorial regimes in the examples of Yuen's body of work that I will engage with in this chapter involves new, unexpected connections, transformations, and lines of flight from common-sense structures of meaning, especially those at work in the West. Again, the analyses will confirm that the countering of territorial regimes is interdependent with the empowering image of femininity.

Yuen Woo Ping and the Film Culture of Hong Kong

When we consider Yuen's work within the context of Hong Kong cinema, and here I am alluding not only to his predecessors but also to his contemporaries, we will find indicative similarities. Particularly relevant is the comparison with the two directors/action choreographers — Sammo Hung and Lau Kar Leung. Both of them, just as Yuen, had a traditional education; Hung was a member of the above-mentioned child troupe Seven Little Fortunes, and Lau was trained by his father, the martial arts master Lau Charn, a student of Lam Sai Wing, the most famous disciple of Wong Fei Hung. For his films, Yuen engaged his father and his brothers; Lau often worked with his adopted brother Lau Kar Fai (who is perhaps best known to the Western audiences from Quentin Tarantino's *Kill Bill:* Volume 1, and Volume 2); and Sammo Hung often worked with his former opera classmates, Jackie Chan, Yuen Biao and Yuen Wah. As I stated in Chapter 1, both of these filmmakers, just as Yuen, are studio-trained directors who followed very similar career path — they started as stuntmen and played small parts in numerous films, after which they became action choreographers, and finally, directors.

All three of them are connected with the famous directors of the golden age of Mandarin martial arts cinema of the 1960s and 1970s produced by the Shaw Brothers. Sammo Hung worked as action-choreographer for (among others) King Hu, on films such as *Fate of Lee Khan/Ying chun ge zhi Fengbo* (1973) and *Dragon Gate Inn*; Lau Kar Leung was Chang Che's action choreographer on his *Golden Swallow* (1969) and *Heroes Two* (1975). Yuen Woo Ping worked with (among others) Chor Yuen, and is credited for action choreography on his *Bastard/Xiao za zhong (1973)* and *Lizard/Bi hu* (1972). Both Sammo Hung and Lau Kar Leung, just as Yuen Woo Ping, were involved in films that featured strong female characters. Hung instructed one of the most popular actresses of that period — Angela Mao — in films *Lady Whirlwind/ Tie zhang xuanfeng tui* (Feng Huang, 1972) and *Hapkido/He qi dao* (Feng Huang, 1972) — as well as in King Hu's above-mentioned *The Fate of Lee Khan*. In this period, Lau Kar Leung trained an actress who would become even more popular than Mao — the legendary Cheng Pei Pei in Cheng's film *Golden Swallow*.

In the late 1970s things started to change in the filmic universe of Hong Kong: a number of young people returned from studying in North America and England, and the (first) Hong Kong New Wave was ready to emerge. The filmmakers who marked this moment were Ann Hui, Patrick Tam, Tsui Hark, and others. In the films of these new filmmakers the center of interest was not traditional China — Hong Kong was the subject and so were the contemporary social and psychological problems. A film culture began to emerge — with cine clubs, magazines and workshops; in 1977 the Hong Kong International Film Festival was established. Most of the New Wave directors began by innovating standard genres; action cinema was slowly giving way to so-called "art cinema." Kung fu comedy, a transitional sub-genre, emerged during this period. Yuen, Hung, and Lau anticipated the transformations, and each one of them contributed in his own way to the revitalization of action cinema, especially of the kung fu genre.

Reinventing the Great Martial Arts Hero

Yuen Woo Ping's big break as a director came with two Jackie Chan vehicles, *Snake in the Eagle's Shadow* and *Drunken Master,* the two films that introduced a completely new version of the legendary kung fu master Wong Fei Hung. This was the first comical version of the great Cantonese hero, an expert of the *hung gar* style, a bonesetter who lived in the late Qing Dynasty and early Republican China in the southern Chinese city of Fushan at the turn of the nineteenth century.[2] Chan's young Wong is immature and disobedient, but his athletic skills are so well-developed that they allow him to play with the kung fu moves and stances without threatening the cultural, philosophical, and ideological function of kung fu as a discipline.[3] The arrival of Jackie Chan on the scene in 1978 as a more comical version of the great martial arts hero was a sign that the martial arts genre was undergoing a transformation; the generic combination of kung fu and comedy confirmed this fact. Chan's humorous account of Wong Fei Hung gave a totally new perspective on the kung fu legend, and at the same time it was drastically opposed to serious martial arts heroes such as Bruce Lee.[4]

Wong passed his skills on to students, and a number of his second- and third-generation disciples could still be found in the 1980s in Hong Kong. One of them, as mentioned, was the famous director and action choreographer Lau Kar Leung.[5] In the series of films from the 1950s to the 1970s, the image of Wong Fei Hung was one of moral virtue and dedication to protecting his nation from the foreign devils trying to exploit China at the end of the nineteenth century. The actor who had monopolized the on-screen presence of Wong Fei Hung and offered an elderly and virtuous version of the legendary hero was Kwan Tak Hing.[6] Before he became a film star, Kwan Tak Hing was an actor in Cantonese operas, hence he was familiar with acrobatics as a necessary component of this type of stage acting. He appears as Wong Fei Hung in Yuen Woo Ping's films *The Magnificent Butcher* and *Dreadnaught*.[7]

While it has often been pointed out that the Wong Fei Hung created by Yuen and Chan is comical and playful, I would like to emphasize the problematic and inadequate figures of authority in Yuen's films. These male figures were quite typical of kung fu comedy in general, as I already noted, Yuen's filmic universe needs to be considered in terms of the cultural context that produced it.

Yuen's films are therefore not an exception, but they are rather exemplary of the characters that circulated in the kung fu comedies of that period. Just as Wong Fei Hung's father, who ultimately needs to be rescued by his son in *Drunken Master*, the threatened male authority figure is a recurring element in each of Yuen's films that I will discuss in the following sections. We will see that in each of the films the ineffective male authority is directly related to the influential position of female characters in the narrative. Keeping with the aims of this study, I will first observe Yuen's and Chan's (re-)construction of the image of Wong Fei Hung in terms of its deterritorializing elements.

Drunken Master: In and Out of Control, Becoming Miss Ho

In the beginning of *Drunken Master,* a middle-aged mother engages in combat with the young Wong Fei Hung, who has taken advantage of her daughter's foolishness, and when caught in the act, tries to blame his unseemly behavior on the girl. This scene, in which the mischievous Fei Hung is defeated by his aunt, a middle-aged woman (the girl's mother), demonstrates that he needs improvement as a person and a fighter (Stills 4.1, 4.2). This mother is portrayed by Linda Lin Ying, who stars in Yuen's *Dance of the Drunk Mantis.*

Thanks to the tradition, a middle-aged actress who is a martial arts expert was available. Conversely, these actresses, trained to deliver intense physical performances, make possible the construction of a certain type of character-image that, with the example of *Wing Chun*, I have described as the empowerment-image. Since this type of female character is bound up with a specific socio-cultural imaginary, there need not be a justification on the level of the story (how can she be such an excellent fighter?),

Still 4.1   Still 4.2

Stills 4.1, 4.2 In Yuen Woo Ping's *Drunken Master* (1978) a middle-aged mother engages in combat with the young Wong Fei Hung (played by Jackie Chan), who has taken advantage of her daughter's foolishness.

because the rules and norms that regulate the film's fabula permit a certain kind of female behavior. Unlike this strong mother in a supporting role, Fei Hung's actual father, a kung fu master himself, does not manage to control his son. From the very opening of the film, Fei Hung behaves in a disobedient and disrespectful manner and mocks his kung fu instructor. We can conclude that he has a problem with authority; when he is told that Sam Seed, the famous kung fu master, will be responsible for his future training, he runs away. Sam Seed catches up with him, but as soon as his first opportunity arises, Fei Hung escapes again.

Simon Yuen, a veteran of the Beijing Opera School and Yuen Woo Ping's father and teacher, plays the role of Wong Fei Hung's drunken kung fu master. In fact, *zui quan* or drunken boxing was part of the real Wong Fei Hung's repertoire. Drunken boxing gives the impression that the fighter is out of control and that he will lose balance at any moment. While this fighting technique presupposes that the combatant only mimics holding and drinking from a cup, in Yuen's comedy Sam Seed drinks constantly, and indeed he cannot function without guzzling large quantities of wine.

Nevertheless, and contrary to our expectations, thanks to his drunken fighting, Sam Seed can beat any opponent. Similarly, what makes the pupil Wong's performance especially comical is his ability to appear completely drunk and hence out of control, while being able to execute his "drunken" techniques with the utmost precision. This type of fighting, pushed to the limits in a kung fu comedy, inevitably has a deterritorializing effect, for it is the flight from logic, reason, and conscious behavior that finally conditions Fei Hung's becoming a capable fighter.

In terms of the narrative, Fei Hung's occasion for transformation finally arises once he realizes that he needs Sam Seed's help. In a chance encounter with a brutal opponent, Fei Hung is heavily beaten and subjected to utter humiliation; he rushes back to his teacher and willingly resumes his training sessions. This is not the first rebellious martial arts student; the most famous "rebel," the one-armed swordsman in the film of the same title (*Dubei Da*, 1967), directed by Chang Cheh, offers a dramatic version of a young fighter's conflict with authority. In Yuen's kung fu comedy, resistance to authority is underscored in particular through Jackie Chan's clownish kung fu, which has also been described as slapstick kung fu.[8]

One specific kung fu stance that causes dispute between the student and the master and causes clownish ridicule is the "Miss Ho" move. Although in Taoist terms the feminine element (yin) is essential for the achievement of complete spiritual and physical balance, Chan's Fei Hung does not blindly follow instructions, but displays instead resistance to his own, potentially feminine side. When his master introduces this stance to him, Fei Hung is skeptical and mocks the move. Even after Sam Seed smacks him and demonstrates the stance several times, Fei Hung refuses to fight in a feminine way. Nevertheless, it is precisely the "Miss Ho stance" that secures his victory in the final duel. Hence, it is only after he gets in touch with his feminine side and incorporates the "female movements" into his fighting that Fei Hung manages to beat the enemy.

It is useful to recall that the two fundamental phases of action in Taoism, yin and yang, serve to designate feminine and masculine. The first of the commandments of the adepts who received Tao teching was to practice non-action and gentleness, or rather, to keep their femininity and never take the initiative. In *The Taoist Body,* Kristofer Schipper explains that the Taoist doctrine inspired by Lao Tzu's teachings — to know the masculine and yet maintain the feminine — "is to become the valley of the world" (Schipper 1993: 128). The physiological practices of nourishing the Vital Principle require that one first realize the female element, which also includes the adoption of a female posture.

Apart from the influence of Taoism, kung fu comedy as a genre draws on the tradition of street acrobatics, the northern-style martial scenes featured in Beijing opera, and even this scene from Yuen's film confirms these connections.[9] It goes a step further however, because the theatricality and the camp aspect of the "Miss Ho" scene, thanks to Jackie Chan's performance, enhances the comical aspect of the film and mocks the tradition (Stills 4.3–4.6).

Young Wong's becoming a master of kung fu remains an ongoing process because he never quite manages to approximate the image of the traditional hero, the virtuous, honorable and respectful young man. Even so, in spite of the fact that he is a rascal who at times questions and refuses to follow his teacher's instructions, in the end he still manages to beat the enemy and save his father's face. In relation to this we can note that there is an acceptance/ affirmation of authority, but the filial behavior of this Wong Fei Hung is expressed on his own terms. If the traditional heroes took the feminine component for granted (as well as the masculine one, for that matter), Chan's and Yuen's Wong Fei Hung is elaborated as sexually aware and ready to negotiate, albeit in a comical way, the representation of masculinity, femininity, and paternity.

Still 4.3

Still 4.4

Still 4.5

Still 4.6

Stills 4.3–4.6   Although Wong Fei Hung initially mocks the "Miss Ho" move, it is precisely this feminine stance that secures his victory in the final duel.

Becoming Mantis: Saving the Father

In Yuen Woo Ping's film *Dance of the Drunk Mantis*, another middle-aged woman (Linda Lin Ying) uses martial arts skills; she is first introduced in a scene where she has to protect herself from extortion and verbal abuse (Stills 4.7–4.10). Even though her husband is frequently away from home, her fighting skills enable this woman to survive on her own. When the husband returns after a long absence, he finds his wife has adopted a son. Yuen Siu Tin resumes his role as Sam Seed, the master of drunken kung fu, and

Still 4.7   Still 4.8

Still 4.9   Still 4.10

Stills 4.7–4.10 An empowering image of femininity is also offered in Yuen's *The Dance of the the Drunk Mantis* (1979) where a middle-aged woman defends herself from extortion and verbal abuse.

as an additional confirmation of the importance Yuen Woo Ping places on the expert performance of physical action, the role of Sam Seed's adopted son Foggy is played by Simon Yuen's actual son Yuen Shun Yee. In this film, then, Yuen Shun Yee, Yuen Woo Ping's brother, and an expert fighter in real life, plays the role of Foggy, the son who is taught kung fu by his mother.

Within the Western imaginary it is unthinkable that an older woman could be a skilled kung fu fighter. In mainstream Hollywood films, female fighters are appearing more frequently, but they are generally young and attractive women.[10] The fact that in Yuen's films middle-aged or older women (*Drunken Master*, *Dance of the Drunk Mantis*) and even a fat woman (*Drunken Tai-Chi*) can be expert fighters capable of defeating arrogant and abusive men is dependent on the connection between narrative and rules and norms that regulate what is imaginable and conceivable. Undoubtedly, this is connected to the representation of both men and women in cinema. The notion that some forms of activity are more appropriate for men and some others for women has its roots in the common-sense understanding of acceptable male and female behavior, the categories which are best expressed in images, stories, and in general fictions.

Proof that such a division of roles is a fiction can be found in the normal state of things in Hong Kong cinema. Women of action commonly appeared in other Hong Kong films of this period. One should recall the female cop movies produced by Sammo Hung — *Yes, Madam!/Huang gu shi jie* (Corey Yuen, 1985), and *Lady Reporter/Shi jie da shai* (Hoi Mang/Corey Yuen, 1989) featuring Cynthia Rothrock and Michelle Yeoh, or *She Shoots Straight/ Huang jia nu jiang* (Corey Yuen, 1990) starring Joyce Godenzi. Jackie Chan was one of the producers for *Inspector Wears a Skirt/ Ba wong fa* (Wellson Chin, 1988). Women of action have also appeared in Lau Kar Leung's films, played by Kora Hui Ying Hung. Hui had a supporting role in Lau's *Dirty Ho/Lantou He* (1979) and *Legendary Weapons of China/Shi ba ban wu yi* (1982), but she had leading roles in his films *My Young Auntie/Zhang Bei* (1981) and *The Lady Is the Boss/Zhangmen Ren* (1983).

In Chapter 2 I argued that the law that determines *what can*, in the first place concerns the level of the fabula. The way a female subject is expressed in a filmic text is closely related with the way the story is told, but it is first of all dependent on some form of understanding of the world such as the following: that the hero needs to be goal-oriented, that happiness entails a union of a heterosexual couple (as is most often the case in classical Hollywood cinema), or, and this is relevant for Hong Kong cinema, that a woman can be a martial arts expert, that she can signify action and even single-handedly save the (fictional) world, as is the case in Yuen Woo Ping's universe.

In *Dance of the Drunk Mantis* the male authority is absent from the house and the fact that the woman is in charge underscores the imbalance of the fictional world. Not only does she have to take care of herself, but she also has to symbolically create a son/ successor by herself. Moreover — and we will see that this is not an uncommon practice — in the absence of the father, the mother (Linda Lin Ying) teaches the son (Yuen Shun Yi) kung fu.[11] The father figure/authority is represented as irresponsible and unreliable, and he tries every possible trick to avoid his paternal duty. The son, Foggy, wants Sam to teach him kung fu, but after Sam repeatedly abuses Foggy's confidence, makes a fool of him and subjects him to painful and humiliating experiences, Foggy cannot bear it anymore and leaves.

A competing kung fu master, Rubber Legs (Hwang Jang Lee), who has come to challenge Sam with his "Drunken Mantis" stance, further complicates the problem of Sam's authority. Sam is heavily beaten in the duel with Rubber Legs, and it is only through Foggy's intervention that he escapes death. On his way to fetch the medicine for Sam, Foggy encounters a ghost-like character/ "the sickness master" (Sai Kun Yam) who offers to teach him kung fu. As in a number of Yuen's other films, the basic Taoist principles are employed, and the ghost teaches Foggy about yin and yang. Foggy is not the only one helping Sam; the mother is also involved in fending off Sam's adversaries. She reaffirms her martial arts expertise when Rubber Legs's student (played by Corey Yuen, another former member of the Little Fortunes) arrives at their house looking for Sam. The kung fu student uses a spear, while she draws a sword. The woman is more skillful; she rips up the young intruder's pants and kicks his behind. When the son Foggy arrives, he takes on the opponent and the adversary is defeated for the second time.

In the final showdown between Sam Seed and Rubber Legs, again, the son arrives just in time to save his father's face. He wins the duel through his transformation into an idiot, by becoming a madman; in so doing, he draws on forces and stances unknown to Rubber Legs. Because the powerful adversary cannot predict the moves, he does not succeed in defending himself. With the help of the mother, the "ghost of Tai Chi," and finally by transforming into a madman, in yet another Yuen Woo Ping film, the face of the father can be saved.

Fat Woman in the Zone of Microfemininity

In *Drunken Tai-Chi*, an overweight middle-aged woman realizes that she is the object of ridicule of a young vendor who has convinced her to don a dress that will supposedly make her look slim. Contrary to all expectations, she turns out to be a skilled kung fu fighter who teaches the imprudent man a lesson. This female character is played by the famous Hong Kong (and Singapore) film and television comedienne Lydia Sum. The hero of this film, Cheng Do (Donnie Yen), who orchestrates this joke, is introduced as an arrogant womanizer who loiters all day and plays pranks. This is Donnie Yen's first film role, and his martial arts skills helped him to secure it. Yen is one of those actors who possess excellent martial arts skills, and aside from playing the role of Wing Chun's sweetheart in *Wing Chun*, he has a leading role in Yuen's *Drunken Tai-Chi* and *Iron Monkey*.[12] Yen's mother is Master Bow Sim-mark, a famed Boston-based tai chi and wu shu instructor. Yen began learning from his mother as soon as he could walk and he soon became a champion competitor on the US tournament circuit.[13]

To increase the comic effect, and playing on the viewers' extratextual knowledge, but especially to confirm the authority of the women fighters, in both *Drunken Tai-Chi* and *Wing Chun,* he plays a man whose combat skills are inferior to those of the main female characters. Interestingly, and comparable to the scene in

Drunken Master where a middle-aged mother teaches the young Wong Fei Hung a lesson, the first to beat up the disrespectful Cheng Do is a fat middle-aged woman (Stills 4.11–4.14).

Still 4.11

Still 4.12

Still 4.13

Still 4.14

Stills 4.11–4.14 In Yuen's *Drunken Tai Chi* (1984), the first to beat up the disrespectful young hero Cheng Do is a fat middle-aged woman.

The fat woman is not the only one who wants to teach Cheng Do a lesson, however. A trap is set for him, but due to a fortunate development of events he escapes unharmed; instead, the attackers are badly hurt. This outcome triggers a pledge for revenge, and a savage-like murderer Killer Bird (Yuen Shun Yee) is hired to do away with the entire Cheng family. Cheng Do's father is an old miser who favors Cheng Do, for he is the older son, and ruthlessly exploits the younger one. He is elaborated as a caricature of a traditional father figure. This unsympathetic father only loves money, and when Killer Bird sets the house on fire, instead of saving himself and his younger son, the father wastes precious time trying to save his treasures. As a result, both of them die in the fire. This tragedy occurs while the older brother Cheng Do is out gambling. He is still in danger though, because the vicious killer is determined to hunt him down.

On the town square Cheng Do accidentally causes damage to the Taoist puppet-master (Yuen Cheung Yan), and since he has no money, the only way he can compensate for the loss is to become his slave. As it turns out, the puppeteer will become Cheng Do's teacher, echoing the legendary Taoist relationship between the ruler (Yellow Emperor) and his sage (considered to be one of the many incarnations of Lao Tzu). They form a pair, puppet and the puppeteer, the medium and his master, which corresponds to the fundamental relationship in Chinese thought (Schipper 1993: 218).

Husband and Wife, Yin and Yang

In the house of the puppet-master we encounter his wife, the fat woman who taught Cheng Do a lesson. Speaking of the socio-cultural imaginary that conditions a certain type of male and female behavior, we need to recall that Taoist masters — the men and the women — are generally married (although not necessarily to each other). As Schipper reminds us, in the school of Heavenly Master the highest level of initiation — the quality of Master — was conferred not on individual adepts, but on couples. In the book of Chuang Tzu there were many women among the initiates. Later, the movement of the Heavenly Master was organized on the basis of absolute equality between men and women, who shared in equal numbers the leadership of the liturgical organization. The Heavenly Masters themselves shared their duties with their wives.[14] The married couple in Yuen Woo Ping's kung fu comedy, *Drunken Tai-*

Chi is in a constant power struggle; we are reminded of the male-female tension in Yuen's film *Miracle Fighters*/Qi men dun jia (1982) where the two characters are elaborated as embodiments of yin and yang.[15]

In *Drunken Tai-Chi,* each spouse wants to appropriate Cheng Do for his/her personal needs. Cheng Do runs away from the bickering couple, but just as Wong Fei Hung in *Drunken Master,* after barely surviving the encounter with the brutal enemy, he realizes he has no other option but to return to their home. The master and his wife are happy to have him back, and this time they treat him as the son they had never had. When they hear about Killer Bird, they both want to teach Cheng Do to fight effectively. The master tells him that he will teach him tai chi, a soft style, to counter the killer's hard style. He explains that tai chi is split into male and female, and his wife knowingly adds, "yin and yang."

At first, Cheng Do finds it difficult to adapt to the soft rhythm and internalize the instructions that recur in several of Yuen's films, in particular *The Tai Chi Master.* In these instances the hero is ultimately taught to use the soft style to counter the immense force of his enemy. Quite typical of martial arts masters, the Taoist couple gives Cheng Do different chores that prove to be useful exercises. In the end, Cheng Do triumphs in the duel against Killer Bird, and a happy surrogate family is formed. Cheng Do gains caring and responsible albeit wacky parents, and the childless couple now has a son.[16]

This is yet another in the series of films where Yuen's creative energy is invested in perfecting the physical performance of the actors, where the plot is a pretext, as David Bordwell states, for a parade of splendors (Bordwell 2000); the story is as simple as it can be, and the cinematography, mise-en-scène, sets, locations and costumes are all in the service of producing spectacular action. I would add, however, that while the story is incredibly simple, the fabula reveals the cultural specificities of an action cinema that cannot be found in the West — a cinema where a fat woman can be in the zone of microfemininity, an embodiment of the empowerment-image, a literal relation of speed and slowness.

Sister's "Laundry Kung Fu": Becoming Brave

The main character of Yuen's film *Dreadnaught* is a coward, Mousy, who is bullied by everyone. To increase the comic appeal, Mousy is played by one of the Seven Little Fortunes, the well-known martial artist Yuen Biao. He runs a laundry business with his sister, but he is easily intimidated and does not manage to collect the money for their services. At home, he argues with his mirror image and threatens the imaginary enemy with his sister. The sister (Li Li Li) is another forceful female character in a supporting role; she is fed up with her brother's cowardice because it is doing damage to their laundry business. Her position as the stronger sibling is already confirmed at the moment she insists that the clothes he is wearing are dirty and need to be washed. Although Mousy disagrees with her, he does not stand a chance against her method of persuasion — their family laundry kung fu. She disrobes him in a matter of seconds (Stills 4.15–4.19).

Ah Foon (Leung Ka Yan), the disciple of Wong Fei Hung, befriends Mousy and tells him he will teach him to be fearless. Mousy wants to become brave, and he also wants to be Wong's student. The imbalance of this fictional world is established through the position of the sister in the narrative as the only authority figure in Mousy's life. He has no male authority figures or role models. Unlike the new "brother"Ah Foon, who helps Mousy gain self-confidence, the sister is elaborated as the one who patronizes him.

The villain in this film is Tam Hing (Phillip Ko) of the Northern Lion Troupe, who wants his competitor, Wong Fei Hung (played by the celebrated actor Kwan Tak Sing), dead. Wong demonstrates

Still 4.15

Still 4.16

Still 4.17

Still 4.18

Still 4.19

Stills 4.15–4.19   In Yuen's *Dreadnaught* (1981), the hero-in-the-making Mousy does not stand a chance against his sister's method of persuasion — their family laundry kung fu.

his expertise as a doctor who practices Chinese medicine, and he is also involved in training a troupe of lion dancers in street acrobatics. In *Dreadnaught*, Wong helps his students in the competition by taking part in the dance. Through Wong Fei Hung, the film combines performing arts, Beijing opera, and martial arts. In fact, the film's finale takes place in an empty theater. Tam Hing hires a hunted criminal named White Tiger (Yuen Shun Yee) to kill Wong Fei Hung. Judging from his behavior, White Tiger appears to be a deranged man; his condition can be related to the death of his pregnant wife who was killed in the clash with the bounty hunters at the very beginning of the film. As another confirmation of female activity in Yuen's films, it is interesting to note that even a pregnant woman (Kam Kar Fung) is depicted as capable of fighting forcefully and challenging her attackers. And indeed, White Tiger's wife does not lose her life in combat; one of the attackers sneaks up on her and stabs her with a knife.

Mousy's friend Ah Foon is killed in a fight against a stylized non-human creature with a body composed of two frontal parts and a head with two faces. The murder is orchestrated by the vile Tam Hing, and when Mousy arrives at the theatre to avenge the death of his friend, Wong Fei Hung soon joins him. When Wong is seriously injured, Mousy has to confront the killer alone. Ultimately, he is confident enough to put his family laundry kung fu to use, and he triumphs.

In this film Yuen makes use of the folklore and theatrical origins of the kung fu comedy. The scene in the theater where we catch a glimpse of a martial artist on stage most directly evokes the intertextual and intermedial character of kung fu comedy (Still 4.20).

It is a highly stylized yet a phenomenal filmic world where the sister and not the brother is the master of the family (laundry) kung fu. In other words, I would suggest that in this film, becoming-brave entails reaching the threshold of microfemininity.

Still 4.20 In *Dreadnaught*, Yuen Woo Ping makes use of the folklore and theatrical origins of the kung fu comedy.

Women of Action Joining Forces with Male Heroes

In spite of the fact that the women in the above examples do not play a prominent role in the development of the narrative, they can nevertheless offer us new insight into the ways in which femininity can be re-imagined. While the examples introduced above certainly confirm the fact that in the fictional worlds of Yuen's films even fat or old women can display authority (albeit on a temporary basis) even more fascinating are the women of action who have a more prominent role in the development of the narrative. In his *Iron Monkey* and *The Tai Chi Master,* the main female character joins forces with the central male character.

Joining Forces with Iron Monkey

In this film, Miss Orchid Ho (Jean Wang) assists the famous Qing Dynasty folk hero Iron Monkey (Yu Rongguang) (Stills 4.21–4.23). In the first instance, Iron Monkey can be understood as the alter ego of the esteemed Doctor Yang, who runs a medical practice with his female assistant. Miss Ho is also involved in his adventures where he steals from the rich and gives money to the poor. Although Iron Monkey/Doctor Yang ultimately teams up with Doctor Wong (Donnie Yen), the father of the legendary kung fu master Wong

Fei Hung (who is just a boy in this film, and actually played by a girl, Tsang Sze Man),[17] in the end of the film Miss Ho saves both of their lives.

Still 4.21

Still 4.22

Still 4.23

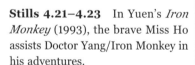

Stills 4.21–4.23 In Yuen's *Iron Monkey* (1993), the brave Miss Ho assists Doctor Yang/Iron Monkey in his adventures.

Because of his commitment to help the poor, Iron Monkey has been compared to the legendary hero Robin Hood. In spite of the fact that in the ballads of Robin Hood, Maid Marian is depicted as a cross-dresser, a good archer, a skilled swordswoman, and Robin Hood's assistant, in the film versions of Robin Hood, Maid Marian is not portrayed as an active woman. Hence, within the Western imaginary even this rare example of a woman of action from the past has gradually been transformed into a passive female beauty.

Who Is the Monkey?

The corrupt officials are taking measures to catch Iron Monkey; they have even secured the services of the monks, but to no avail. The main reason they cannot catch him is because of his superb martial arts skills. They finally decide to arrest anyone who is skilled in martial arts or who is in any way connected with the term "monkey." Doctor Wong and his young son, Fei Hung, arrive in town amid these arrests, and as excellent kung fu fighters, before long they are escorted to jail. I have already suggested that Yuen Woo Ping's art as a filmmaker is interdependent with his genius as an action choreographer; Wong Fei Hung's umbrella fight as an adult in Tsui Hark's *Once Upon a Time in China* starring the Chinese martial arts champion Jet Lee and choreographed by Yuen himself, echoes the breathtaking impact of the scene from *Iron Monkey* where the young Wong Fei Hung also fights with an umbrella.[18]

Still 4.24   Wong Fei Hung as an adult in Tsui Hark's *Once Upon a Time in China* (1991), with Yuen Woo Ping as the action choreographer.

Still 4.25   Tracing similarities on the intertextual level: Wong Fei Hung as a boy, fighting with an umbrella in Yuen's *Iron Monkey.*

The officials let Doctor Wong go because he insists that he can find the actual Iron Monkey, but they retain the boy as collateral. It is inevitable that the two men, who are both doctors and phenomenal kung fu masters, will ultimately join forces. This is a gradual process, however, that involves other characters that mediate between the two men, notably Wong's son Fei Hung, Officer Fox (Yuen Shun Yee), the only trustworthy government official, and most importantly, Miss Orchid Ho.

Renegotiating Masculinity: Becoming Iron Monkey

Doctor Wong tries to maintain the image of a traditional authority/father figure, and his conservative attitude is most evident in the relationship with his son. When Fox comes to report that the legate officer plans to arrest Wong and Yang and that they need to go into hiding, Fei Hung starts crying. His father puts on a stern face and says that a man should be as strong as steel and that he should not shed tears easily. But when the father turns away from his son we see that he is also crying — the father and the son wipe off their tears synchronously. We see here two faces of masculinity; it is possible to conclude that masculinity is being renegotiated through the comical aspect of the narrative, as crying in a comedy is certainly less threatening to the traditional image of masculinity. Finally, through the renegotiation of a historical figure such as Wong Fei Hung, history itself is being renegotiated. (This process of "rewriting history" through the image of Wong Fei Hung will be radicalized in Tsui Hark's *Once Upon a Time in China*.) Furthermore, as mentioned, unlike Doctor Yang, Doctor Wong is not a rebellious person; in the beginning of the film he even condemns Iron Monkey's actions. Nevertheless, as the film progresses he is increasingly on the side of the rebels.

Renegotiating Femininity: Becoming Iron Monkey

Indeed, there are three "Iron Monkeys" in the film's closing — Yang, Wong and Orchid Ho. In the final spectacular showdown, when Yang and Wong are about to fall into flames and burn to death, Orchid throws them long poles to help them save themselves from the fire.

It is interesting to note that Miss Ho herself had been rescued by Doctor Yang at a time when she was a completely different woman, and in the course of the film her history is revealed in a flashback: While she is nursing young Wong Fei Hung back to health, she remembers the time presumably after she has given birth. This is undoubtedly her time of bondage and oppression; we see her wretched past self, seriously ill, weak, and bed-ridden. She recalls a scene where her brutal master kills the baby and orders her to get out of bed. Although on the verge of collapsing, she finds the strength to attack the murderer and is ready to face the fatal consequences. Fortunately, Doctor Yang/Iron Monkey intervenes. He offers gold in exchange for Miss Ho's freedom.

Unlike the more typical scenarios where a woman rescued by a man retains the role of a passive object, Doctor Yang's honorable deed has led to Miss Ho's emancipation. This is manifested most radically through her becoming-Iron Monkey.

The Betrayed Monk and the Abandoned Wife Join Forces

In *The Tai-Chi Master*, the main female character, Siu Lin (Michelle Yeoh) teams up with the Buddhist monk Junbao (Jet Li), whose spiritual brother and companion Tianbao (Chin Siu Ho) have betrayed him and have chosen to side with the powerful Royal Eunuch (Lau Shun). Siu Lin herself has been betrayed by her husband, who has gone away and married the sister of the eunuch. As a result of these equally dismal circumstances, Siu Lin and Junbao join forces in the fight against evil. The film is set during that era of Chinese history that precedes the decline of the Ming Dynasty, when thousands of troops led by Royal Eunuchs are in the service of collecting taxes from the suffering population.

As far as the role of the eunuchs in the Ming Dynasty is concerned, it has been argued that their influence in matters of state had detrimental consequences.[19] In spite of the fact that within the traditionalist view, eunuchs are the scapegoats for an autocratic political system, these emasculated yet most influential of men are typically portrayed as power-hungry despots.[20] Due to their high rank within the system, eunuchs had access to offices, libraries, and treasuries inside and outside the Forbidden City. They could come into possession of secret weapons, including magical swords; they also knew the hiding places of sacred scrolls that could provide them with knowledge about the most lethal and powerful martial arts stances.[21] Only those who mastered the art of fighting, the swiftest and the most courageous of warriors, the rebels or members of secret societies, could survive encounters with these tormented tyrants — Siu Lin and Junbao are such magnificent warriors.

Mortgaging the Organ: Becoming Powerful

Deleuze and Guattari's concept of a Body without Organs (BwO) is quite pertinent here, considering that eunuchs are bodies without organs in the most literal sense. Deleuze and Guattari explain that the BwO is the field of immanence of desire, the plane of consistency specific to desire, with desire defined as a process of production without reference to any exterior agency, whether it is lack that hollows it out, or pleasure that fills it (Deleuze and Guattari 1983). Basically, following the thought of Deleuze and Guattari, it would be ideal if we could "become" a BwO, turn ourselves into a BwO, unaffected by structures that want to organize our desire. This, of course, is something we can only strive for because there is always something that wants to uproot desire.

The eunuchs' literal becoming-BwO does not immediately imply the countering of a territorial regime because within this context, becoming-eunuch at the same time corresponds to becoming-powerful. What conditions their becoming-powerful is the mortgaging of their penises — not in the Lacanian/symbolic sense, but again, in the literal sense.[22] Let us recall that Jacques Lacan strengthens the relationship between the Oedipus complex and language through the paternal signifier — what he calls the "Name-of-the-Father." This is the determining signifier in the history of the subject and the organization of the larger symbolic field. Lacan also introduces the term phallus to indicate the cultural privileges, and positive values that define male subjectivity within patriarchal society. In "Field and Function of Speech and Language," Lacan suggests that in order to acquire cultural privileges the male subject mortgages "that pound of flesh," that is, he mortgages the penis for the phallus. Quite similar to the Lacanian subject, the eunuchs acquire cultural privileges in exchange for their penises; by mortgaging their organs, hundreds of them managed to secure jobs in the Emperor's palace. One of those BwO's is also the Royal Eunuch, the representative of an oppressive authority that rules in this filmic narrative. Many believed that the only solution to their troubles would be to start an uprising and kill this BwO.[23]

Junbao and Siu Lin become involved with the rebels' cause, whereas Tianbao ultimately sides with the oppressors of the people. To prove his loyalty to the Royal Eunuch, Tianbao betrays his friends and even gets the woman who loves him, Little Melon (Fennie Yuen Kit Ying), killed. This frustrates the plan of the rebel groups in the area to assassinate the Royal Eunuch. Although Siu Lin and Junbao put up a heroic fight, due to Tianbao's deceit they are outnumbered by the government troops.

Defending the Inner World: Becoming Tai Chi Master

Tianbao's behavior confirms the fact that the idea of brotherhood is deeply corrupted. Junbao is shocked when he is betrayed by his spiritual brother. Haunted by feelings of guilt for trusting him with the rebels' plan, Junbao withdraws into seclusion.

He finds *The Book of Qi* that his old master had given him and he starts practicing tai chi. The exercises that were the origin of today's Taoist gymnastics and *tai chi chuan* (boxing of the Highest Ultimate) can be taken as analogous to Deleuze and Guattari's idea of "becoming"; the exercises are called the Dance of the Five Animals, and such a method of harmony and well-being is a martial art for the defense of the inner world. Speaking of the connections with Deleuze and Guattari, becomings can be expressed in the alternation of yin and yang, as an alternation of movement and rest, speed and slowness.[24] Taoists give priority to the human body over social and cultural systems; according to Taoist thought, our bodies are formed through the coagulation of energies, *chi,* and this coagulation obeys a transformational dynamic inscribed in time. The fusion of yin and yang at the center comes in a moment of self-mastery.[25] This moment of self-mastery that does not hinge on social and cultural systems can be understood as becoming-BwO in the most productive sense, a BwO that can defy gravity and common sense.[26]

A Superwoman against the Eunuch

With the guidance of an old Taoist master and the support of Siu Lin, Junbao regains the inner strength that will help him excel in the fight against evil, first against the Royal Eunuch and then against Tianbao. To accomplish this, however, he will need the help of his female friend Siu Lin.

The evidence that corruption has penetrated into every realm of the society, including religious life, is confirmed in the scene where Master Liu is in a procession led by Buddhist monks. The procession is interrupted by the sudden attack of Siu Lin and Junbao. The breathtaking action that follows once again confirms the influence of Beijing opera on kung fu film, for this is another scene elaborated as a dance of a Deleuzian BwO rather than as a plausible fight.[27] Siu Lin revolves rapidly on the ground so as to keep pace with the energetic rhythm of the music, while the Royal Eunuch is spinning in the air, fighting from above, and defying gravity, his face directed down towards the camera. This extraordinary performance is typical of a Royal Eunuch; one only has to remember the Royal Eunuchs in both versions of *The Dragon Inn* (*Long men ke zhan,* King Hu, 1966 and *Xin long men ke zhan,* Raymond Lee, 1992). As mentioned earlier, only the most exceptional fighters could overpower these folded BwO's, and one of them is clearly Siu Lin.[28] Just as the Eunuch, she zooms and rockets through the air as a true superwoman, graceful, powerful and invincible (Stills 4.26, 4.27).

Still 4.26   Still 4.27

Stills 4.26, 4.27 Siu Lin fights the powerful Royal Eunuch in Yuen Woo Ping's *Tai Chi Master* (1993).

Siu Lin defeats the Eunuch and takes him hostage. When he is confronted with the state of things, Tianbao proves to be even more atrocious than the government authorities. Although the Royal Eunuch has accepted him as his protégée, instead of complying with Siu Lin's and Junbao's demands, Tianbao kills the Eunuch and assumes the highest position of authority. Nevertheless, due to Siu Lin's mediation, Tianbao loses the support of his soldiers. Ultimately, with his newfound spiritual force, Junbao defeats Tianbao, his cruel and treacherous other.

Becoming Female Rebel

In *The Tai Chi Master* there are three female characters who display expertise in martial arts; apart from the main female character Siu Lin there is another woman, Little Melon, fighting on the side of good. The third woman, Siu Lin's adversary, is the sister of the Royal Eunuch who married Siu Lin's estranged husband. Within this cultural imaginary it is not unusual to encounter female characters in the resistance; martial arts novels such as those of Jin Yong/Louis Cha celebrate women rebels, famous examples being the One-Armed Princess from his novel *The Deer and the Cauldron* or the female rebels from his *Fox Volant of the Snowy Mountain*.[29]

In Chinese history, women rebels were members of secret sects and groups that had their own blood oaths, religious rituals and brotherhoods. Once recruited into these ranks women were given a prestige and a function in a society largely denied to them. According to some accounts, women who joined Triad lodges in advance of their husbands could claim precedence within the household over their own spouses. In Chinese high society and particularly in non-Han, non-Confucian families, a certain freedom was accorded to women — ambiguous, but nonetheless effective.

Thus, the daughters of Taoist "Boxers" received a military education like their brothers, and took part in political struggles as rebels or "bandits" fighting against feudal law. Female brigades of the Taiping were instructed in the art of war (Spence 1990). It is thus logical that the appearance of women fighters does not require special narrative justification and explanation.

When we first encounter Siu Lin she is lost and desperate, searching for her estranged husband. Once she finds him she learns that he is now married to a powerful wicked woman, the sister of the Royal Eunuch, and does not want anything to do with Siu Lin. When attacked by her husband's new wife, Siu Lin proves to be an excellent fighter, more skillful than her arrogant adversary. She defeats her female opponent and at the same time delivers an incredible performance balancing on poles as an acrobat. In spite of her great skills as a fighter she nevertheless appears powerless against her husband. We witness a scene where this pathetic, emasculated man beats Siu Lin and humiliates her in public while she does not make an attempt to defend herself.

In *The Tai Chi Master* just as in *The Iron Monkey* (and in *Wing Chun*, for that matter) the female character undergoes a process of transformation and emancipation. In *Wing Chun* we learn about Wing Chun's past from a pretext (and a flashback), in *The Iron Monkey* we find out about Miss Ho's past from a flashback. In *The Tai Chi Master*, Siu Lin is introduced in a contradictory way as both strong and weak; she is clearly independent and capable of defending herself but she desperately needs emotional support, for she is on the verge of destroying herself drowning her sorrow in alcohol. After joining forces with Junbao, Siu Lin becomes a rebel fighter.

Evidently, these female heroes from Yuen's films have a similar history. They have suffered abuse in the past and therefore the circumstances forced them to "find their body without organs," to both literally and metaphorically become-superwomen.

Becoming Progressive: Emancipated Woman Saves the Hero

In Yuen's universe there are also cases of active women who provide a negative image of femininity, women who are in the service of evil such as the sister of the Royal Eunuch, the new wife of Siu Lin's husband. Ruthless female fighters appear again in Yuen's *The Heroes Among Heroes/So qi er.*[30] They belong to the White Lotus sect that is helping the corrupt imperial prince (Stills 4.28–4.31).

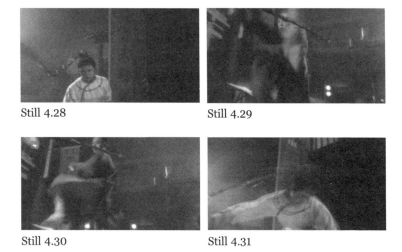

Still 4.28   Still 4.29

Still 4.30   Still 4.31

Stills 4.28–4.31 In Yuen Woo Ping's *Heroes Among Heroes* (1993), the female White Lotus sect is helping the corrupt imperial prince, confirming again the fact that representation of femininity in Hong Kong cinema has multiple faces.

The prince sides with the opium smugglers and hires the sect to eliminate So Chan (Donnie Yen), who is a potential threat to the traitors.

Beggar So is the central protagonist of this filmic narrative and he would eventually join forces with the main female character, Princess Yi Teh-Tai (Fennie Yuen Kit Ying). Although the princess is not a woman warrior like Wing Chun or Siu Lin, who render the sense of empowerment through action, she offers an empowering image of femininity through her progressive ideas and emancipated behavior. The first sign that she may be an emancipated woman is her Western appearance, that is, her attire. More importantly, as we soon find out, her ideas do not conform to patriarchal norms. She engages in numerous worthy causes with the overall aim of educating people, especially women. These possibilities are also a part of the cultural norm; in wealthy families, feminine power was homologous to the power of the fathers. This made it possible for Chinese women intellectuals raised in the West to identify with European suffragettes.

For example, the two famous Soong sisters of Guomintang both made their political debuts during that period — one married Sun Yat Sen and then became honorary Chairman of China beside Mao; the other married Chiang Kai-shek.[31] In *The Chinese Women*, Julia Kristeva writes, "Marked by the bourgeois liberation, by the ideas of 4th May, by the Chinese 'suffragette' movement, by the West, whose language they fluently spoke — whether or not they were daughters of the upper classes, they wanted to rise above their condition as women by means of proletarian universalism, in which the cause of women was but among many" (118).

The Inadequate Authority Figure Revisited

In *Hero Among Heroes*, the father of So Chan, Beggar So (Kwan Hoi Shan) is married into his late wife's family, and his word does not seem to count. His arrogant spinster sister-in-law (Sheila Chan), who lives in the same household, constantly bullies him.[32] His inadequacy as a father figure is confirmed in the fact that there is another "father" in So Chan's life, Wong Fei Hung (Wong Yuk) his *si fu* (his kung fu master) whom he refers to as "Dad."

The issue of problematic authority is further conveyed through the 12th Prince, Xiong Xin Xin, who is involved in the opium trade. The already-mentioned White Lotus gang, a dangerous sect of female fighters, guards the Prince's transactions. Via the royal family the film also brings up the issue of race; specifically, on one occasion the Prince says that the royal family must not mix with the Han people, and he condemns Yi Teh Tai's relationship with So Chan. The opposition between the despotic/foreign authority and the honorable Han Chinese people is underscored by juxtaposing the Manchu Prince with representatives of the Han Chinese such as the legendary hero Wong Fei Hung and Officer Lam. More precisely, we are reminded here that the opium trade flourished under the Qing Dynasty of the Manchus. When Officer Lam wants to ban opium for the sake of the country, the Prince advises him to resign. The Manchu/Qing Dynasty is thus obviously portrayed as working against the interests of the Chinese people.

The Woman as the Progressive Potential of the Society

While the Prince represents the negative, decadent aspect of the royal family, Princess Yi The Tai, the emancipated woman, generally demonstrates women's progressive potential in the society. She teaches women to write and runs a women's club and a newspaper, and even organizes a campaign to ban opium. The Princess appears to be much wiser than the central male character, So Chan, who is even tricked by the Prince into giving in to opium and falling under his control. When So Chan is in his deepest crisis, weak from his addiction and having witnessed the brutal murder of his *si fu*, the Princess helps him to get back on his feet again. Just as Princess Yi Teh can be perceived as the vital potential of China and the country's savior, as it were, So Chan can be seen as the embodiment of the Chinese condition of those times — he is weak, old-fashioned, gullible, and helpless.[33] Nevertheless, his recovery and his ultimate willingness to avenge his kung fu master with the help of Wong Fei Hung, and his readiness to engage in the fight against the Prince and the opium trade, allude at the same time to the positive prospects of the country. Crucial for a positive resolution is the redistribution of power; the weak father can hardly help his son, and even the great master and hero Wong Fei Hung is not able to prevent the actions of the enemy of the people, the 12th Prince, on his own. As mentioned earlier, the key to the positive outcome is progress and emancipation, and these qualities are embodied into the main female character.

Tai Chi 2: Female Characters Saving the Hero

As in *The Hero Among Heroes*, the main female character in *Tai Chi 2* has been exposed to influences from the West, and she too behaves in a non-traditional way. In both films, the opium smugglers, as representatives of the most negative image of the West, are juxtaposed with the positive image/influence of the West via a beautiful, young, and intelligent woman. In *Tai Chi 2* there are actually two strong female characters, the mother (Sibelle Hu) of the main character, Hawk (Jacky Wu), and the girl he is in love with, Rose/Yeung Wan (Christy Chung). Although the father of the hero is a great kung fu master (Billy Chow), the mother teaches the son the ways of the world (especially the Western world). In that respect, both female characters represent the progressive side of this fictional world.

While the father is introduced as the highest expert in martial arts, the mother is a wise woman who has a very important place as a diplomat and a mediator — between the traditional and the new, between the East and the West. Her role is subtle, yet incredibly influential. The father, as the formal authority in the household, is the one who sets the rules; he forbids the son to leave the house and forces him to study. In that sense, Hawk emblematizes isolation. Nevertheless, when the father beats Hawk for going out without permission, the mother is angry and she "beats" the father.

Rose studies abroad, she is dressed in Western-style clothes, and just as Hawk's mother, she is emancipated. We first meet her at a ritual where she protests against vicious customs such as sacrificing virgin girls to please the King of Dragons. She also refuses to marry the man she was promised to unless they share the same ideas. With a group of young Chinese Westerners, she distributes propaganda leaflets that promote democracy and science. These rebels also criticize the government for relinquishing Hong Kong. The Chinese Westerners tell Hawk that he has to cut off his long braid if he wants to join them, but when they realize that Hawk's braid is an effective weapon, they turn up wearing fake braids and ask Hawk to teach them the "pig-tail stance."

Just as Hawk's father is too seeped in tradition and very self-oriented, we learn that Rose's father is even more inadequate — he is a weak servant of the authorities and an opium addict. In fact, one of the biggest tasks that Hawk and Rose need to accomplish is to help her father to beat his opium addiction. The problem of the weak male authority extends further, for the guards too lack the spirit to learn martial arts to protect their country.

Hawk is very open to influences from the West; thanks to his mother, he is learning English, and she also teaches him to dance the tango. Most importantly, he does not feel threatened by a strong and emancipated woman; he is happy to accept her invitation to a ball. In the ballroom, Rose asks Wing (Mark Cheng), the man she was promised to, to dance, but he does not know how. He has to step aside and watch Rose dance with Hawk, who successfully combines martial arts moves with tango. As in Tsui Hark's *Once Upon a Time in China*, the potential of China to transform is personified through the female character. In Tsui's film, Wong Fei Hung's Aunt Yee/"Thirteenth Aunt," just as Rose in *Tai Chi* 2, dresses in Western-style clothing and speaks fluent English. The female character underscores the importance of learning from the West in order for China not to fall behind.

Still 4.32   In Yuen Woo Ping's *Heroes Among Heroes* or *Tai Chi 2*, the women are elaborated as more emancipated than the men. Similarly in Tsui Hark's *Once Upon a Time in China*, Aunt Yee (Rosamund Kwan) is the one who teaches Wong Fei Hung about the handshake.

Still 4.33

Still 4.34

Stills 4.33, 4.34   She also teaches him to dress like a man from the West.

Still 4.35   To attend a theatre performance, Aunt Yee dresses up as a man.

In *Tai Chi 2*, the opium smugglers kill Wing, clearly a much less vital character than Hawk who does not display the capacity to change with the times. Hawk is blamed for the murder, but fortunately the group of Chinese Westerners witnessed the entire event and they clear up the matter.

In the final showdown, Hawk has to confront Smith (Darren Shahlavi), a British citizen and the chief coordinator of the opium smuggling. The duel between a Chinese and a Western man evokes the issues of body politics and both masculinity and "musculinity." When Smith's upper body is revealed, we see that he is very built up, yet a skinny boy such as Hawk is able to defeat him. The only way Smith can possibly win the duel is if he uses a gun. He ultimately takes a hostage to save himself, but Rose resolves the problem by shooting Smith in the head. She tells Hawk she practiced shooting in the US. Evidently, the traditional martial arts hero does not suffice in the new historical circumstances. As we learn from Yuen's film, he needs to join forces with an emancipated woman (Stills 4.36–4.38).

I have compared two situations from Yuen's films from Tsui Hark's *Once Upon a Time in China* to additionally underscore the fine line between Yuen's status as a director and his engagement as an action choreographer. Throughout his career Yuen was directing his own films, but he also worked with directors such as Tsui Hark, who invested their energy not so much in perfecting

Still 4.36

Still 4.37

Still 4.38

Stills 4.36–4.38   Confirming again the similarities on the intertextual level, the main female character in Yuen's *Tai Chi 2* has also been exposed to the influences from the West. Her expertise in shooting a gun resolves the ultimate problem in the film. The main male character, Wing, like Wong Fei Hung in Tsui's *Once Upon a Time in China*, wears accessoires from the West.

the action (this was left to Yuen Woo Ping) but in meeting the standards of the Hollywood film industry. In that sense, Yuen can be observed as a link between the golden age of the Shaw Brothers production, via the Hong Kong New Wave, and the era of the polished productions of Tsui Hark, where special effects experts from the West are imported to work on Hong Kong films. Bringing Western standards to the industry and rejuvenation of the Hong Kong production framework had occurred already with the New Wave, and Tsui is considered the key modernizer and innovator.

Yuen Woo Ping, on the other hand, has remained a constant connection, making possible the action images of both the old and the new.

Conclusion: The Power of Fabulations

What *can* be imagined in Yuen Woo Ping's films are women fighters, female characters elaborated as subjects of action and as the last two examples show, emancipated women in general. Structures of meaning expressed on the level of the story, such as the idea that a woman can save the world, are closely related with the vision on the level of the fabula and this vision is linked with specific cultural determinations. The structures of meaning at work in Hong Kong films put the cultural fixations of the Western imaginary under pressure and generate an unprecedented sense of female empowerment. It is in this sense that I have described Yuen's films as the "art of empowering women."

These examples of strong and emancipated women belong to the same universe as Wing Chun. Powerful women as a recurring motif enable us to ultimately draw specific conclusions about Yuen Woo Ping's filmic universe.[34] This imaginary inhabited by women of action inspires stories of female empowerment. What makes these fantasies of female empowerment possible are fabulations related to specific cultural and social norms. While the strategies of storytelling could be described as simplistic, what needs to be taken into consideration is precisely the imagination required to conceive these fictional worlds. In that respect, the women in these films can be taken as examples of "new possibilities" for these are fictional worlds that operate according to an alternative legal sensibility to the dominant standards. These films work in such a way as to counter the territorializing regimes and enable alternative universes to come "out of a shadow by a beam of light." The prime example of this world of speed and slowness, movement and rest, of becoming as a way to get rid of the organism, is the universe of Yuen Woo Ping.

5

Re-thinking Conceptual Tools, Re-framing Imaginary Solutions

Putting Pressure on Feminist Film Theory (Once Again)

The types of imaginary solutions that can occur in a given narrative, such as the idea that a woman can save the world, are bound up with the legal sensibility of a concrete socio-cultural imaginary. As we are constantly reminded, within the Chinese cultural context, alternative structures of signification are at work, and the potential for imagining alternative female characters acquires new dimensions. This presupposes also that the notorious Freudian division between the sexes — active/male versus passive/female — needs to be complemented with the models of signification at work in Chinese society. For example, the Taoist rule of contraries traceable in the myriad of filmic narratives infers interdependency rather than the strict separation of masculine and feminine forces.

If we go back to the 1960s, to King Hu's *A Touch of Zen,* which can be taken as exemplary of a trend of Hong Kong action heroines, we will find that the woman is active and a skilled fighter, while the man, her unwed husband and the father of her child, on many occasions acts as an observer and supports her cause. In this film, a government officer who has come to arrest the woman interrupts this idyllic situation. The man, completely ignorant of her extraordinary fighting skills, makes an attempt to defend her. The woman steps forward ready to defend herself and reaches for her dagger. He is absolutely stunned when he realizes that the woman with whom he has just spent the night is an expert fighter (Stills 5.1–5.3).

Still 5.1

Still 5.2

Still 5.3

Stills 5.1–5.3   In King Hu's *A Touch of Zen* (1969) the woman is active and a skilled fighter, while her male partner is an observer.

A Touch of Zen was produced in 1969; it was screened at the Cannes film festival in 1971, two years before Laura Mulvey's seminal article "Visual Pleasure and Narrative Cinema" was written, and four years before it was published in the journal *Screen*. Let us recall that the article takes as its starting point the way film reflects socially established interpretation of sexual difference that controls images, erotic ways of looking and spectacle. Especially relevant is Mulvey's argument that an active/passive heterosexual division of labor controls the narrative structure of classical Hollywood films. There is a split between spectacle and narrative, which supports the man's role as the active one who advances the story, making things happen. When it comes to Hong Kong films, an opposition between activity and passivity, or the tension between spectacle and narrative do not necessarily refer to the division between the sexes. As I have already noted, "spectacle" has to do with spectacular action, which in many martial arts films compensates for the straightforward storytelling techniques.

In "Afterthoughts on Visual Pleasure and Narrative Cinema," Mulvey has revised her views but she still relies on Freud's ideas when the active solution for the crisis of femininity is concerned (Mulvey 1989). For Freud, as Mulvey reminds us, "femininity is complicated by the fact that it emerges out of a crucial period of parallel development between the sexes; a period he sees as masculine, or phallic, for both boys and girls. The terms he uses to conceive of femininity are the same as those he has mapped out for the male, causing certain problems of language and boundaries to expression. These problems reflect very accurately, the actual position of women in patriarchal society" (1989: 30). Feminist film theorists extended Mulvey's research, and representation of femininity is being addressed from multiple perspectives. Mary Ann Doane, for example, introduced the concept of the female body in its relation to the psyche (shifting the emphasis from psyche and image) (Doane 1982, 2002); Teresa De Lauretis explored sexual and social indifference in Western culture as well as lesbian representation, especially the connection between the body, language and meaning (De Lauretis 1994); bel hooks focused on the representation of race in film (hooks 1992); Carol Clover discussed gender crossing in horror films and argued that women in slasher films are "transformed males," challenging thereby gender specific theories of identification (Clover 1992). In terms of the new approaches to psychoanalytic film theory that can be brought to bear on a filmic text such as *Wing Chun*, I find Judith Butler's concepts especially productive. I have already mentioned the relevance of her theory of gender as performative (rather than biological) when discussing queering of gender images through cross-dressing in *Wing Chun*. Her view on the structure of gender as unstable, coincides with Deleuze's and Guattari's ideas on de/re-territorializing of meaning.

I do not want to imply that the complexities related to the representation of femininity in Hong Kong films need necessarily follow the framework that I am proposing. In fact, these issues are being addressed from different positions; for example, in their piece entitled "Of Executioners and Courtesans: The Performance of Gender in Hong Kong Cinema of the 1990s," Jenny Lau and Augusta Lee Palmer analyze what they call the "courtesans" of art cinema and the "executioners" of genre cinema. They explore the socio-political and historical terms under which the potentially strong female protagonist is constructed (Lau and Lee Palmer 2003). One of my aims, however, particularly in this concluding chapter, is to reflect on the limits of the theoretical concepts forged for the measure of Western imaginary, the limits that oblige us to keep searching for new points of vision.

Putting Pressure on the Father-Universe: Hollywood Style

Psychoanalytic approach to film implied also that the specific structuring of the narratives has been theorized in terms of the Oedipalization of the subject. According to the psychoanalytic scenario, the son's "destiny" is to take the father's place. In the new Hollywood this process is principally no longer at work, but the father and the son nevertheless remain the two central protagonists of the symbolic universe; instead of internalizing the authority of the father, the son has to recreate this authority.[1] The thematizing of paternal authority can be brought to bear on Jacques Lacan's notion of the Law of the Father. While the male characters can easily engage in an intersubjective exchange, this is not readily the case when female characters are concerned. In keeping with the woman's mythological role as a monster, or in Lacanian terms, the object of plenitude, the female characters often end up stuck in between the subjective exchange of the male characters. The active solution to the crisis of femininity is becoming more and more open to the female characters of the mainstream cinema, but these are principally action-heroines in the service of patriarchy. They are the action-heroines who can perform "masculine" tasks: they are physically strong and display high combat skills; they can act as leaders, and maintain or restore the law and order of patriarchy. More importantly, they are inserted into the Oedipal trajectory, implying that they are initiated into the father-universe.[2]

Putting Pressure on the Father-Universe: Hong Kong Style

The examination of Yuen's body of work in Chapter 4 demonstrates in general that the authority figures in his films are represented as powerless or worthless. The fathers are not able to endorse their authority, and other mentors have to take on their role; in *Drunken Master*, the vagabond Sam Seed steps in; in the *Dance of the Drunk Mantis*, both the mother and "the ghost of tai chi" figure as substitutes for the father. Hence, (in place of the father) the young hero has to rise to the challenge and defeat the sinister yet mighty adversaries. In the context of the crisis of the father/male authority, the opportunity inevitably arises for female characters to take charge. In the film *Dreadnaught,* the father is absent and the sister of the cowardly hero is the one who orders him around. The problem of authority is equally pronounced in *Tai Chi 2,* where one father is too traditional and has a difficult time adapting to the new historical circumstances, and the other father, a government official addicted to opium, is even more ineffective. In *The Tai Chi Master*, the authority is first personified by Master Liu, the corrupt Royal Eunuch, and later by the power-hungry monk Tian Bao. In *The Miracle Fighters*, possibly the most stylized and theatrical of Yuen's films, the action is set in 1663 (and in 1677), the time of the Manchu rule. The baby Prince is abducted, and the one who plans to establish his evil rule via the Prince is the Evil Sorcerer. It is such a disturbing time that even the "yin" and "yang" embodied in the two bickering characters are under threat.

Similarly, in *Wing Chun*, the men are weak or display some kind of shortcoming and the lack of (masculine) power is even underscored literally in the duel where Wing Chun's opponent loses his private parts. In the fictional world where female characters play such a prominent role and where the highest authority is personified by a female character, the emerging question is: what is the role of male characters in this symbolic universe? Or more importantly yet, if the diegetic universe of *Wing Chun* functions according to the Law of Wing Chun, what is the status of the Law of the Father that has haunted the fundamental concerns of feminist film theory and defined and governed discussions on the representation of femininity?

De/Re-territorializing Desire

I am referring to Jacques Lacan's notion of the Law of the Father, which governs the symbolic order (Lacan, 1977).[3] Lacan's concept of the "symbolic" was inspired by the writings of the French anthropologist Claude Lévi-Strauss.[4] His ideas are crucial for Lacan's theory of the subject in that he proposes a close connection between the structuring agency of the family and language. The family, as part of a symbolic network, is defined by a set of symbolic relations that always transcend the actual persons; these are cultural positions and need not have a biological/natural connection. Lacan further strengthens the relationship between the Oedipus complex and language through the paternal signifier — which he calls the "Name-of-the-Father."

For Lacan, this is the determining signifier in the history of the subject and the organization of the larger symbolic field. Lacan also introduces the term *phallus* to indicate the cultural privileges and positive values that define male subjectivity within patriarchal society, to which the female subject has no access. Basically, this aspect of Lacan's theory has provoked and continues to provoke feminist criticism; in "Field and Function of Speech and Language," Lacan suggests that, in order to acquire cultural privileges, the male subject mortgages "that pound of flesh," that is, he mortgages the penis for the *phallus*. As feminist critics have argued, Lacanian theory turns the woman into the foreclosed element, as the "constitutive outside" of the Law of the Father, for she lacks that which the male subject renounces to enter the symbolic order.

When we consider a non-Western cultural imaginary populated with female warriors, a diegetic world that draws on the Taoist concept of the subject as dependent on the continuous exchange between feminine and masculine energy — yin and yang — or if we consider stories where Confucian doctrines clash with Buddhist teachings, as is also the case in *Wing Chun*, or just as importantly, if we take into account the castrated men who literally sacrificed "that pound of flesh," it is clear that the woman warrior cannot be observed as dependent on the paternalistic symbolic order theorized by Lacan. It is not difficult to conclude that Wing Chun's universe is contingent on an alternative symbolic network based on alternative fabulas and worldviews. While Lacan's concept of the symbolic urges us to consider Wing Chun as a cultural position defined by a set of symbolic relations, at the same time, precisely the fact that Wing Chun is a cultural position makes it difficult to place her into a theoretical framework based on symbolic relations that inform Lacan's psychoanalytic concepts.

Cultural Positions and Narrative Representation

As I have emphasized in previous chapters, and in keeping with Geertz's notion of "legal sensibility," stories and imaginings are bound up with a law that is rejoined to other cultural formations of human life such as religion, the division of labor, or history. I have also suggested that the characters' vision is bound up with a worldview that exceeds the fictional world of the film, and that it is dependent on critical and philosophical concerns of the outer world. More specifically, and in keeping with the narratological approach, I have related this vision to the level of the fabula.

As I have explained, in order to recount the fabula of *Wing Chun* we have to go back to the time when Wing Chun herself was threatened by the bully and was forced to take refuge in the Buddhist temple where she learned kung fu. The fabula of the film relies on the legend, the myth of a woman warrior who gave the world a new martial art, which means that we need to consider the events that exceed the fictional world of the film. Therefore, the fabula of *Wing Chun* is predicated on the specific pre-text; it draws on the events that *precede* the actual process of storytelling. What makes both the story and the main female character plausible is precisely this pre-text that informs the fabula; it refers us to the cultural context that is, the socio-cultural imaginary that conditions the Universe of Wing Chun.

Clearly, the fabula of *Wing Chun* offers an emphatically positive image of femininity, and it challenges the Lacanian symbolic universe where the Law of the Father is at work. As argued earlier, it can be taken as an example of creative fabulation, and it displays a "legal sensibility" that is difficult to find in the Western imaginary; it features a female character from the distant past who is emancipated in ways that defy the common understanding of women's liberalization through social movements. It is precisely this positive image of femininity that reveals an incredibly powerful yet simple imaginary solution to the crisis of femininity. In that respect, the fabulations at work in the filmic universe of Yuen Woo Ping can broaden our conception of the images of both femininity and masculinity, and we can come closer to understanding that there are alternative implications (to those of the Western imaginary) regarding the feminization of men, as well as — what could be described as — women taking on a masculine role.

This is a universe where, together with Yuen Woo Ping's women of action, a plethora of gender-bending characters existed, such as those in *Swordsman* and *Swordsman II,* for example. In *Swordsman*, the Sacred Scroll is stolen from the Forbidden City and Royal Eunuchs are searching for the perpetrator. The scroll contains mystic teachings of martial arts, and the one who gets a hold of it can acquire supernatural powers such as seeing through objects and exerting energy across great distances. Interestingly, as it happens in *Swordsman II,* the possibility to acquire absolute power becomes related with castration, that is, with renouncing one's sexuality. In this film, the evil General Fong has come into possession of the sacred scroll and uses its scriptures to obtain supernatural powers in his quest to control China and the world.

Following the scriptures, he has to perform self-castration and assumes the name Asia the Invincible. Fong is played by Brigitte Lin and in the course of the film s/he transforms from man into a woman. Eunuchs can here be observed in terms of their deterritorializing function. In *Swordsman II* becoming-eunuch is a transitional phase in the process of becoming Asia the Invincible. When s/he becomes a woman, Asia the Invincible falls in love with the young swordsman Ling, who is actually the worst enemy of her prior (male) self — the despotic, power hungry General Fong. Ultimately, the transsexual subversive organism is constructed through the decomposition of the autocratic organism.

While in *Swordsman II* Asia displays heterosexual tendencies, in *East is Red* she functions more like a transsexual lesbian super hero/villain. Obviously, the problem of power and authority, just as the question of Asia's sexuality, remains open for negotiation. I would suggest that s/he emerges as the embodiment of Deleuze and Guattari's idea of sensory becoming as "the action by which something or someone is ceaselessly becoming other (while continuing to be what they are)" (Deleuze and Guattari 1991: 177).

The Law of Wing Chun

The types of imaginary solutions that can occur in a given narrative, such as, that a woman can save the world, are bound up with the legal sensibility of the concrete socio-cultural imaginary. What this means is that the symbolic universe governed by the Law of the Father should be seen as just one possibility and not as a norm, because there are various alternative signifiers and alternative universes. In that respect, Butler's reconceptualization of Lacan's law of signification is relevant for the discussion on the Law of Wing Chun; it underscores the fact that the law of signification is not predetermined or fixed (Butler 1993).[5] As far as the study of

Wing Chun is concerned, at stake is not only the possibility of investing the space of the excluded (from the Lacanian symbolic ordered by the Law of the Father) with meaning, at stake is the possibility of conceiving an altogether separate symbolic order, or even multiple symbolic orders. As a subject, Wing Chun is dependent on her specific cultural position, implying her position in the fabula/the symbolic universe.[6] It is this cultural position that defines her as a subject on the cultural *screen*.[7] Elsewhere, I have argued that narration is the precondition for the invention of new symbolic universes, and one of the crucial concerns of my project was to explore the discursive potential of the (female) space of extraterritoriality.[8] New universes can come into being to the extent that alternative signifiers are enabled to compete with the paternal signifier. The Law of Wing Chun engages our capacity to envision a different kind of (especially) female existence, and it is an occasion for alternative subjectivities to come into being.

This approach to narrative differs, for example, from Bordwell's *Narration in the Fiction Film* because the emphasis is on the structural aspects of the fabula, whereas Bordwell focuses principally on narration, as dependent upon a perceptual-cognitive account of the spectator's activity. Following Bal's definition of narrative, at the outset I stated that the fabula makes describable a segment of reality that is broader than that of narrative texts only (Bal 1997). This assertion needs to be considered as bound up with the notion of culture and the ways in which culture affects the concept of subject. In his anthropological studies, Geertz has demonstrated that what defines an individual in a given society can vary greatly according to different cultures. It is in this context that we can comprehend Bal's assertion that the very notion of subjectivity, so central in narratological considerations of agents in the fabula, cannot be given a fixed, universal meaning.

As a type of female subject in a specific narrative, Wing Chun is dependent on a cultural position; this position enables a universe in which she is the highest authority. It is a universe with spectacular female action contingent on creative fabulation rather than intricate storytelling techniques. Following Deleuze and Guattari's line of thought, I have described creative fabulation as the art of countering dominant structures of meaning invested in the "empowerment image." Hence, female authority is not confirmed through the process of telling, but as the analysis of *Wing Chun* repeatedly demonstrates, through the art of empowering.

Notes

Chapter 1   Yuen Woo Ping and the Art of Empowering Female Characters

1   Actually, he started his film career with small roles as a martial artist in the Wong Fei Hung classics of the 1960s. I return to this in Chapter 4.

2   See for example Roger Garcia's "The Doxology of Yuen Woo Ping" in *A Study of the Hong Kong Martial Arts Film, The 4 th Hong Kong International Film Festival* (137–140). See also Stephen Teo's section "Kung fu and Modernization".

3   In *Butterfly Murders*, for example, Tsui Hark announces his interest in the supernatural potential of *wuxia pian* which can be bolstered up with special effects, a new trend in martial arts films that he would further explore in the projects of his Film Workshop in the 1990s. In *Ashes of Time* Wong Kar-wai interweaves the formal elements of "art cinema" with the martial arts genre, experimenting with the new ways of de/constructing space and time and accordingly, the characters' subjectivity.

4   Both Tsui and Tam are considered "New Wave" directors *par excellence*, whereas Wong is regarded as a representative of "New Hong Kong Cinema." See Yau and Abbas.

5   In Chinese, an action choreographer is referred to as action director.

6   In spite of its sophisticated story world and special effects, what made *The Matrix* truly exceptional was the combination of Hollywood's high-tech effects and Yuen's martial arts choreography. Similarly, without Yuen's imaginative action, Lee's "high brow" *Crouching Tiger, Hidden Dragon* would not have had such a deep impact on the audiences (especially in the West). During the press screening of Lee's film at the Cannes Film Festival the first scene that provoked the critics' applause was the scene choreographed by Yuen where Michelle Yeoh is chasing Zhang Ziyi across a wall.

7   To be discussed further in Chapter 4.

8   I am referring to the festival and art house films, and also to European cinema.

9   As these are related to certain aspects of the Hong Kong film industry, particularly its mode of production. When it comes to cinematic art, style in principle refers to the systematic or inventive use of cinematic devices as these are related to the process of narration.

10   In the conclusion of his *Narration in the Fiction Film*, David Bordwell states that his theory being an account of narration, will not necessarily help define matters of narrative representation or narrative structure. In contrast, in the study of Wing Chun and the work of Yuen Woo Ping I am placing the emphasis precisely on narrative representation and narrative structure as it is related with the cultural imaginary.

11   See "Hong Kong Cinema and the Art of Countering Territorial Regimes," in *Discernments: Deleuzian Aesthetics*.

12   Women were expected to follow the strict code of the three Obediences — at home obey your father, after marriage obey your husband, after your husband's death obey your son.

13   Speaking of legendary Beijing Opera stereotypes where a female character is made to be both a pretty heroine and a military hero, the most famous one is certainly Hua Mulan (Fa Mulan in Cantonese pronunciation). In *the Legends of China* series presented five years ago at the Hong Kong Cultural Center there was a magnificent opera

The Ladies of the Great Yang Family, based on a heroic story of twelve women warriors of the Song Dynasty, all of whom are skilled in martial arts, and the head of the family is the grandmother. For the examples of women warriors in martial arts novels, see for example Jin Yong's (Louis Cha) *Deer and the Cauldron* and *Fox Volant of the Snowy Mountain*. See also *Classical Chinese Tales of the Supernatural and the Fantastic* edited by Karl Kao, in particular the story "Li Chi, the Serpent Slayer."

14 I will say more about this reversal of the Freudian division between the sexes; in Hong Kong cinema women are often portrayed as active whereas the men are passive

15 Different sources on the year of production — 1925 and 1930.

16 I am referring to Princess Leia from Star Wars. Generic clash (and a temporal paradox) comes from the reference to the past event that happened a long, long time ago juxtaposed with futuristic space vehicles.

17 We have to add that these fantasy narratives with exaggerated physical types are often derived from comic books, within imaginary locations.

18 George Lucas' statement regarding his decision to set the *Star Wars* story in outer space is indicative of this: "I researched kids' movies and how they work and how myths work; and I looked very carefully at the elements of films within that fairy tale genre which made them successful. [...] I found that myth always takes place over the hill, in some exotic far-off land. For the Greeks it was Ulysses going off into the unknown, for Victorian England it was India or North Africa or treasure islands. For America it was out West. There had to be strange savages and bizarre things in an exotic land. Now the last of that mythology died out in the mid-1950s, with the last of the men who knew the old West. The last place left 'over the hill' is space." Quoted in *Movie Brats* (133). It was out there in a galaxy far, far away, that scary monsters, androids and princesses could be in charge.

19 See Yvonne Tasker, *Spectacular Bodies: Gender, Genre and the Action Cinema*.

20 This assertion is inspired by Michel De Certeau's concept of history in his *The Writings of History*.

21   I am referring in the first place to Laura Mulvey's "Visual Pleasure and Narrative Cinema" in *Visual and Other Pleasures*.

22   In fact, when she defeats the chief bandit she earns the title "Mom"; and as the "mother" of thieves she orders them immediately to be good.

23   Jen and Jade Fox in Ang Lee's *Crouching Tiger, Hidden Dragon* is a failed master/pupil relationship.

24   Imaginary solution as a notion refers to Claude Levi Strauss only to the extent that it evokes myths and mythologizing.

25   See Susan Jeffords, *Hard Bodies*, and *Remasculinization of America*.

26   This presupposes a systematic analysis of the aspects and elements of narrative but it also urges critical awareness and theoretical reflection.

27   Speaking of the films of the late 1960s and early 1970s, I am referring in particular to the films of King Hu and Chang Che.

Chapter 2   Structuring the Narrative: Becoming "Wing Chun"

1   Needless to say, the separation of the fabula from the story or the text is only theoretical because the functioning of the narrative involves the simultaneous interaction of all three layers.

2   The Buddhist nun is referred to as "Wu May" in the Mandarin version and "Ng Mui" in the Cantonese version.

3   I say more about Jackie Chan and kung fu comedy in Chapter 4.

4   See my "The Art of Countering Territorial Regimes: Women Warriors, Wicked Eunuchs and Soccer Players from Shaolin" in *Discernments: Deleuzian Aesthetics*.

5   I return to this in Chapter 4.

6   Fong Sai Yuk is a historical figure and a legendary kung fu fighter.

7   In my analysis of new Hollywood cinema, I have demonstrated that this tendency is connected with reinstituting patriarchal myths and generally improving the male subject. See my *Subjectivity in the New Hollywood Cinema: Fathers, Sons and Other Ghosts*.

8   See *Subjectivity in the New Hollywood Cinema*.

9   I have introduced this approach in *Subjectivity in the New Hollywood Cinema*.

10 Edward Branigan, for example, principally defines focalization on the basis of the characters' vision and opposes this to non-focalization, hence to non-vision.

11 See my *Subjectivity in the New Hollywood Cinema*.

12 Such as Fa Mulan, for example.

13 I am referring to Deleuze's *Cinema 1* and *Cinema 2*. Movement-image as conceptualized by Deleuze inferred the films of classical Hollywood and it was opposed to the time-image that pertained to the art-house films or more precisely the post-Second World War European film movements such as Italian neorealism or the French New Wave.

Chapter 3   The Power of Female Action

1 For the discussion on style see, for example, Bordwell's *Narration in the Fiction Film*.

2 Also, many filmmakers came from Beijing opera academies, including Yuen Woo Ping.

3 As noted, the loss of Wing Chun's feminine self in Yuen's film is also a certain disruption of this character-type.

4 Simon Yuen died in 1980, during the shooting of Woo Ping's film *The Magnificent Butcher*.

5 According to Yen, Yuen would work an entire month on one fighting scene. This meant hardcore training from five thirty in the morning until late at night, fighting all day, throwing the same kick or punch over and over again. The aim was to achieve thirty continuous moves, which also implied that the action was filmed in one wide shot. There is no doubt that the performers were put under enormous pressure, and as Donnie Yen confesses, he felt abused mentally and physically and wanted to quit after the first month.

6 Besides fast-paced punching drills and aerial kicking techniques, *wu shu* players learn how to use a wide range of Chinese weapons, so Li has a broad array of techniques at his disposal.

7 Starred in *The Sword* by Patrick Tam, and also numerous martial arts films.

8 During the filming of this scene a double was supposedly used for Wing Chun, as Yeoh had been badly injured.

Chapter 4   The Universe of Yuen Woo Ping

1   See *Shaolin Ten-Animal Form of Kwan Tak Hing*.

2   *Hung gar* is one of the fighting arts that originated from Hunan's legendary Shaolin Temple.

3   See Garcia's "The Doxology of Yuen Woo Ping."

4   Wong was the legendary martial arts instructor of the early twentieth-century Southern China who established the Wong School of martial arts, a style which has become indigenous to the Guangdong region and to the Hong Kong film industry.

5   Lau Kar Leung directed the legendary *36 Chambers of Shaolin*.

6   This was not the first revisionist Wong, however; the first young version appeared in Lia Chia-liang's *Challenge of the Masters*, 1976, in which the character is figured as a reverential mirror of his older self.

7   The main character in Yuen's film *The Magnificent Butcher* was also a historical figure, Wong Fei Hung's student, the butcher Lam Sai Wing. Lam's tales of his master's adventures inspired a series of stories published in a local newspaper. These stories led to the film *The Story of Wong Fei Hung* (1949) which inspired more than seventy Wong Fei Hung films (1949–1970), the longest-running series in cinema history.

8   Jackie Chan has expressed admiration for the kings of film comedy such as Buster Keaton and Harold Lloyd and he has referred explicitly to scenes from their films.

9   And from stage adaptations of episodes from the story of Monkey King.

10   A possible exception is Demi Moore in the sequel of *Charlie's Angels: Full Throttle*, although she plays an attractive professional in the film, rather than the mother of practically an adult.

11   This need not be related to the absence of the father; Donnie Yen was taught martial arts by his mother and Sammo Hung by his grandmother.

12   He also stars in Yuen's *In the Line of Duty*.

13   He later expanded his repertoire to include techniques from various martial arts.

14 "During the ritual of ordination they were supposed to unite their registers, that is, their respective spiritual forces. These registers did comprise the names and symbols of yin and yang energies. This showed that each human being possessed both masculine and feminine elements [...] when the cosmic energies were all there, the adepts would undress and loosen their hair — in ancient China, both men and women had long hair worn in a knot. In the dioceses there were as many female as male masters. This balance was fundamental, even in the practice of perfection, inasmuch as the highest degree of initiation — that which qualified the adept for the rank of master — could only be obtained by a man and a woman together, as a couple. Celibacy was unthinkable." In *The Body of Tao* (150).

15 Speaking of the manifestation of yin and yang, it may be useful to recall the postmodern filmic version of these two interdependent poles, in Wong Kar-wai's *Ashes of Time*. In this film Wong introduces a character called Murong Yang, played by the cult gender-bending actress Brigitte Lin. It turns out that Yang has a "sister" named Yin who wants her "brother" Yang killed. Yang, in turn, wants the man who betrayed Yin killed. The hired killer/narrator is confused and realizes that Yin and Yang are actually two persons in one. He explains that behind these two identities someone is hidden with a wounded soul.

16 Moreover, with the death of the vicious murderer, his little son is orphaned; as the final confirmation of Cheng Do's maturation and potential formation of a new parent-child relation, the film ends with Cheng Do in the nursery visiting Killer Bird's son.

17 Although men played female roles in Beijing opera, in the early days of cinema, women played male roles because cinema was considered a low art.

18 In fact, it would be possible to construct Wong Fei Hung intertextually by mapping out the body of work of Yuen Woo Ping.

19 The fall of the Ming Dynasty in 1644, when the last Ming emperor committed suicide, led to the advent of non-Chinese rulers — the Manchus — and the establishment of the last dynasty in China, the Qing. In the last stage of the Qing Dynasty, China lost the Opium War, and in 1842 the British gained possession of the Island of Hong

Kong. Thus the downfall of the Ming Dynasty can be taken as the onset of foreign invasions. See, for example, Mary M. Anderson, *Hidden Power: The Palace Eunuchs of Imperial China*, and Henry Tsai Shi-shan, *The Eunuchs of the Ming Dynasty*.

20 The first time a eunuch appeared as a character in a martial arts film was in King Hu's *Dragon Inn*.

21 This is regularly the case in martial arts novels such as *The Deer and the Cauldron*.

22 Deleuze and Guattari state that every time desire is uprooted from its field of immanence a "priest" is behind it, and that actually psychoanalysis with its Oedipal structures or the Law-of-the-Father can be understood as a figure of a priest (1983b).

23 Deleuze and Guattari point to the "three body problem": 1) the full BwO on the plane of consistency, 2) empty BwOs on the debris of strata destroyed by a too violent destratification and 3) cancerous BwOs in a stratum that has begun to proliferate (1996: 163).

24 Yang which goes up, can for instance be pictured as a young boy, a dragon, fire, the sky, clouds, the sun, a horse, smoke, or dawn, whereas yin, which descends, is often represented as a girl, a tiger, water, the earth, rain, a tortoise, the moon or an ox. In *The Body of Tao* (152).

25 In love or in artistic creation, one may find it in calligraphy, in poetry, dance, or in all other forms of art. Once accomplished, this oneness is abandoned as a sacrifice and sublimated (159).

26 "Chinese Taoist treatises — the formation of a circuit of intensities between female and male energy, with the woman playing the role of the innate and distinctive force (yin) stolen by or transmitted to the man in such a way that the transmitted force of the man (yang) in turn becomes innate, all the more innate: an augmentation of powers. The condition for this circulation and multiplication is that the man must not ejaculate. It is not a question of experiencing desire as an internal lack, nor of delaying pleasure in order to produce a kind of externalizable surplus value, but instead of constituting an intensive body without organs, Tao is a field of immanence in which desire lacks nothing and therefore cannot be linked to any external or transcendent criterion" (1996: 157).

27   Deleuze and Guattari state that there is a long procession of BwO's; apart from the schizo body, the drugged body and the masochist body, the BwO is also full of gaiety, ecstasy and dance. Each person should find his/her version of a body without organs (1996: 150).

28   According to Deleuze and Guattari, the BwO is opposed not to the organs but to that organization of the organs called the organism. "The BwO howls, they've made me an organism! They've wrongfully folded me! They've stolen my body!" Eunuchs can be understood as bodies without organs that have been turned into an organism, that have come to stand for an oppressive system.

29   Indicative are these passages from Luis Cha's *Fox Volant of the Snowy Mountain*:

> The lady went by the name of Sign Tian. Though she was young, she had already made a name in the Martial Brotherhood of the border region. As her beauty was matched by sharp intelligence and quick wit, the elder members of the Liaodong Martial Brotherhood had given her the title of Glistening Sable. The sable can make great speed on snowy ground, and is sharp and intelligent. (10)

> At length, Fox asked Orchid, not without surprise in his voice, "I understand that your father is the Invincible Under the Sky. Why did he not transmit to you his esoteric martial feats? I have heard that both genders in your house have equal entitlement to the Miao's Swordplay, as the esoteric techniques of your family are passed on to all male and female descendants alike. (229)

30   One of the girls uses her braided ponytail as a weapon, which is actually the crucial weapon of the main hero in the film. In Chang Cheh's *Slaughter in Xian,* the fight with the braided ponytail is used as part of a theater performance.

31   Michelle Yeoh played Soong Ai Ling.

32   Although a beauty in real life in this film she has an unflattering appearance.

33   In the films of the "Fifth Generation" filmmakers, woman is the embodiment of the Chinese condition. This was most pronounced in the films of Zhang Yimou where the leading female role was played by Gong Li. See Rey Chow's *Primitive Passions*.

34   Yuen Woo Ping's *In the Line of Duty* films feature women of action but in this study I focused exclusively on the films in which action is situated in the past.

Chapter 5   Re-thinking Conceptual Tools, Re-framing Imaginary Solutions

1   See my *Fathers, Sons and Other Ghosts: Subjectivity in the New Hollywood Cinema.*

2   In *Spectacular Bodies: Gender, Genre and the Action Cinema,* Yvonne Tasker offers an account of the recent history of the action-heroine. Tasker describes the action cinema of the1980s as a "muscular cinema." Taking into consideration films such as *Red Sonja, Long Kiss Goodnight, Strange Days, Speed, Twister, Terminator 2,* and *Blue Steel,* for example, Tasker adds that "musculinity" is not limited to the male body. While the film *Thelma and Louise* demonstrates the impossibility of escaping the laws of patriarchy, films such as *Blue Steel, Silence of the Lambs,* and *GI Jane* radicalize the extent to which women are constrained to appropriate both "musculinity" and "masculinity." See also Hilary Radner's "New Hollywood's New Women: Murder in Mind — Sarah and Margie," in Steve Neal and Murrey Smith (eds.), *Contemporary Hollywood Cinema* (London, New York: Routledge, 1998) and Sharon Willis's "Combative Femininity: *Thelma and Louise* and *Terminator 2,*" in *High Contrast: Race and Gender in Contemporary Hollywood Film* (Durham and London: Duke University Press, 1997).

3   In terms of Lacan's methodological distinction between the psychic fields, a brief definition is as follows: while the imaginary designates the relation between the ego and its images, the symbolic produces the subject through language and realizes its closed order by the Law, that is, the Law of the Father. The third field Lacan introduces is the real. The real forms the residue of all articulation which escapes the mirror of the imaginary as well as the grids of the symbolic. It is neither symbolic nor imaginary, and it can be understood as a foreclosed element. It stands for that which is lacking in the symbolic order. See Laplanche and Pontalis.

4   In brief, Lévi-Strauss has suggested that the family is the agency by means of which an entire symbolic network can be elaborated. In *Elementary Structures of Kinship*, Lévi-Strauss argues that the rules of kinship and marriage (incest taboo) create the social state by "reshaping biological relationships and natural sentiments, forcing them into structures implying them as well as others, and compelling them to rise above their original characteristics" (490). Lévi-Strauss ultimately emphasizes the importance of language in securing that all the members of a group inhabit the same psychic territory.

5   Butler is advocating the necessity of acknowledging the universal term, ideology, as a site which is open to contest, but she is also insisting on the possibility of subverting the universal term through repetition. According to Butler, what one takes as a political signifier is itself a settling of prior signifiers. A political signifier implicitly cites the prior instances of itself, drawing on the phantasmatic promise of those prior signifiers. Repetition can have a subversive function because it presupposes a return. Butler argues for a site of political contestation which can be understood as a space of analysis where "woman" as a prescriptive model for female subjectivity becomes open for re-negotiation. This presupposes that woman's status as a "stain" of the symbolic needs to be considered in terms of a temporary linguistic unity.

6   This is the argument I elaborated in *Fathers, Sons and Other Ghosts*.

7   Kaja Silverman introduced the term "cultural screen" in her *The Threshold of the Visible World*.

8   I explore this in the chapter "What Can She Know, Where Can She Go: Extraterritoriality and the Symbolic Universe," in *Subjectivity in the New Hollywood Cinema*.

Filmography

Films by Yuen Woo Ping

Dance of the Drunk Mantis (1979) */Nan bei zui quan/Laam bak chui kuen*
Dreadnaught (1981) */Yong zhe wu ju/Yung che miu gui*
Drunken Master (1978) */Zui quan/Jui kuen*
Drunken Tai Chi (1984) */Xiao tai chi/Siu taai gik*
Heroes Among Heroes (1993) */So qi er*
In the Line of Duty *(1989) /Huang jia shi jie zhi IV: Zhi ji zheng ren*
Iron Monkey (1993) */Shao nian Huan Fei Hong zhi tie ma liu/Siu nin*
    Wong Fei Hung ji tit ma lau
Magnificent Butcher (1979) */Lin shi rong*
The Miracle Fighters (1982) */Qi men dun jia*
Snake in the Eagle's Shadow (1978) */She xing diao shou/Se ying diu sau*
Tai-Chi Master (1993) */Tai ji zhang san feng*
Tai Chi 2 (1996) */Tai ji quan*
Wing Chun (1994) */Yong Chun*

Referenced Films

Alien (Ridley Scott, 1979)

Aliens (James Cameron, 1986)

Alien III (David Fincher, 1992)

Alien Resurrection (Jean-Pierre Jeunet, 1997)

Ashes of Time (Wong Kar-wai, 1994) */Dong xie xi du/Dung che sai duk*

Bastard (Chor Yuen, 1973) */Xiao za zhong*

Butterfly Murders (Tsui Hark, 1979) */Die bian/Dip bin*

Charlie's Angels: Full Throttle (McG, 2003)

Come Drink With Me (King Hu, 1966) */Da zui xia*

Crouching Tiger Hidden Dragon (Ang Lee, 2000) */Wo hu cang long/Ngo fu chong lung*

A Deaf and Mute Heroine (Wu Ma, 1971) */Long e jian*

Dirty Ho (Lau Kar Leung, 1979) */Lantou He*

Dragon Gate Inn (King Hu, 1967) */Long men ke zhan*

Dragon Inn (Raymond Lee, 1992) */Xin long men ke zhan*

The Empire Strikes Back (Irwin Kershner, 1980)

Fate of Lee Khan (King Hu, 1973) */Ying chun ge zhi Fengbo*

Fong Sai Yuk (Corey Yuen, 1994) */Fang Shi Yu*

Golden Swallow (Chang Cheh, 1968) */Jin yan zi*

Hapkido (Feng Huang, 1972) */He qi dao*

Heroes Two (Chang Cheh, 1974) */Fang shiyu yu Hong xiguan*

Inspector Wears a Skirt (Wellson Chin, 1988) */Ba wong fa*

Kill Bill: Volume (Quentin Tarantino, 2003)

Kill Bill: Volume 2 (Quentin Tarantino, 2004)

The Lady Is the Boss (Lau Kar Leung, 1983) */Zhangmen Ren/Chang men jen*

Lady Reporter (Hoi Mang/Corey Yuen, 1989) */Shi jie da shai*

The Lady Swordfighter of the Jiangnian (Shang Guanwu, 1930)/ *Huangjiang nüxia*

Lady Whirlwind (Feng Huang, 1972) */Tie zhang xuanfeng tui*

Legendary Weapons of China (Lau Kar Leung, 1982) */Shi ba ban Wu yi*

Lizard (Chor Yuen, 1972) */Bi hu*

The Matrix (Wachowsky Bros, 1999)

The Matrix Revolutions (Andy and Larry Wachowski, 2003)

Mulan (Tony Bancroft, Barry Cook, 1998)

My Young Auntie (Lau Kar Leung, 1981) */Zhang Bei/Cheung booi*

Once Upon a Time in China (Tsui Hark, 1991) */Wong Fei Hung*

The One-Armed Swordsman (Chang Che, 1967) */Dubei Dao*

She Shoots Straight (Corey Yuen, 1990) */Huang jia nu jiang*

The Sword (Patric Tam, 1980) */Ming jian/Ming jim*

Star Wars (George Lucas, 1977)

The Temple of the Red Lotus (Chui Chang Wang/Hung Hsu Tseng, 1965) /
    Jiang hu qi xia/Tsan hong tsu

Terminator (James Cameron, 1984)

Terminator 2: Judgment Day (James Cameron, 1991)

A Touch of Zen (King Hu, 1969) */Hsia nu/Hap lui*

Yes, Madam! (Corey Yuen, 1985) */Huang gu shi jie*

Bibliography

Abbas, Ackbar (1997). *Hong Kong: Culture and Politics of Disappearance.* Minneapolis: University of Minnesota Press.

Anderson, Mary M. (1990). *Hidden Power: The Palace Eunuchs of Imperial China.* New York: Prometheus Books.

Aristotle (1982). *Poetics.* Translated with introduction by James Hutton. New York: Norton.

Bal, Mieke (1994). *On Meaning-Making: Essays in Semiotics.* Sonoma: Poleridge Press.

———— (1997). *Narratology, Introduction to the Theory of Narrative.* Toronto: University of Toronto Press.

Berry, Chris (ed.) (1991). *Perspectives on Chinese Cinema.* British Film Institute.

Bordwell, David (1985). *Narration in the Fiction Film.* London: Routledge.

———— (1997). "Aesthetics in Action: Kung Fu, Gunplay and Cinematic Expressivity," in Law Kar (ed.), *Fifty Years of Electric Shadows.* Hong Kong: Hong Kong International Film Festival/Urban Council, 81–9.

———— (2000a). *Planet Hong Kong: Popular Cinema and the Art of Entertainment.* Cambridge, MA; London: Harvard University Press.

——— (2000b). "Richness Through Imperfection: King Hu and the Glimpse," in David Desser and Poshek Fu (eds.), *The Cinema of Hong Kong: History, Arts, Identity.* Cambridge, New York and Oakleigh, Melbourne: Cambridge University Press, 113–6.

Branigan, Edward (1984). *Point of View in the Cinema: A Theory of Narration and Subjectivity in Classical Film.* New York: Mouton.

Bren, Frank (1998). "Fighting Woman: Cheng Pei Pei and King Hu Legacy," *Metro* 113/114: 81–5.

Brown, Nick et al. (ed.) (1994). *New Chinese Cinemas: Forms, Identities, Politics.* Cambridge and New York: Basic Books.

Butler, Judith (1990). *Gender Trouble: Feminism and the Subversion of Identity.* New York, London: Routledge.

——— (1993). *Bodies That Matter: On the Discursive Limits of Sex.* New York, London: Routledge.

Cass, Victoria (1999). *Dangerous Women: Warriors, Grannies and Geishas of the Ming.* Lanham, Boulder, New York, Oxford: Rowman and Littlefield Publishers, Inc.

Cha, Louis (Jin Yong) (1996). *Fox Volant of the Snowy Mountain,* trans. O. Mok. Hong Kong: Chinese University Press.

——— (1997). *The Deer and the Cauldron,* volumes 1–3, trans. J. Minford. Hong Kong: Oxford University Press.

Chow, Rey (1995). *Primitive Passions: Visuality, Sexuality, Ethnography and Contemporary Chinese Cinema.* New York: Columbia University Press.

Clover, Carol (1992). *Men, Women, and Chain Saws: Gender in the Modern Horror Film.* Princeton, NJ: Princeton University Press.

De Certeau, Michel (1988). *The Writing of History,* trans. Tom Conley. New York: Columbia.

De Lauretis, Teresa (1994). *The Practice of Love: Lesbian Sexuality and Perverse Desire.* Bloomington, Indiana: Indiana University Press.

Deleuze, Gilles (1983). *Cinema 1: The Movement-Image,* trans. H. Tomlinson and B. Habberjam. London: The Athlone Press.

——— (1989). *Cinema 2: The Time Image,* trans. H. Tomlinson and R. Galeta. London: The Athlone Press.

Deleuze, Gilles and Felix Guattari (1983). *Anti-Oedipus: Capitalism and Schizophrenia,* trans. R. Hurley, M. Seem, H. R. Lane. Minneapolis: University of Minnesota Press.

———— (1994). *What Is Philosophy?* trans. G. Burcell and H. Tomlinson. London: Verso.

———— (1996). *Thousand Plateaus: Capitalism and Schizophrenia,* trans. Brian Massumi. London: The Athlone Press.

Desser, David and Poshek Fu (eds.). *The Cinema of Hong Kong: History, Arts, Identity.* Cambridge, New York and Oakleigh, Melbourne: Cambridge University Press.

Doane, Mary Ann (1982). "Film and the Masquerade: Theorizing the Female Spectator." *Screen* 24 (September–October 1982): 74–87.

———— (2002). "Woman's Stake: Filming the Female Body," in E. Ann Kaplan (ed.), *Feminism and Film.* Oxford, UK: Oxford University Press.

Freud, Sigmund (1955). *The Standard Edition of the Complete Psychological Works of Sigmund Freud*, trans. James Strachey. London: The Hogarth Press.

Garcia, Roger (1980). "The Doxology of Yuen Woo Ping," in Lu Shing Hon (ed.), *A Study of the Hong Kong Martial Arts Film.* Hong Kong: Hong Kong International Film Festival/Urban Council, 121–34.

Geertz, Clifford (1983). *Local Knowledge: Further Essays in Interpretive Anthropology.* New York: Basic Books.

Hong Kingston, Maxine (1977). *The Woman Warrior: Memoirs of a Girlhood Among Ghosts.* London: Picador.

Hong Kong International Film Festival (4th) (1980). *A Study of the Hong Kong Martial Arts Film*, ed. Lau Shing-hon and Tony Rayns. Hong Kong: Urban Council.

Hong Kong International Film Festival (5th) (1981). *A Study of the Hong Kong Swordplay Film (1945–1980)*, ed. Lau Shing-hon and Leong Mo-ling. Hong Kong: Urban Council.

hooks, bell (1992). *Black Looks: Race and Representation.* Boston: South End Press.

Hunt, Leon (2003). *Kung Fu Cult Masters: From Bruce Lee to Crouching Tiger.* London and New York: Wallflower Press.

Jeffords, Susan (1989). *The Remasculinization of America: Gender and the Vietnam War.* Bloomington: Indiana University Press.

———— (1996). *Hard Bodies: Hollywood Masculinity in the Reagan Era.* New Brunswick, NJ: Rutgers Uiversity Press.

Kao, Karl S. Y. (ed.) (1985). *Classical Chinese Tales of the Supernatural and the Fantastic: Selection from the Third to the Tenth Century (Chinese Literature in Translation)*. Bloomington: Indiana University Press.

Kristeva, Julia (1986). *About Chinese Women*, trans. Anita Barrows. London: Marion Boyars Publishers.

Lacan, Jacques (1977). *Écrits, a Selection*, trans. A. Sheridan. New York, London: W.W. Norton and Company.

Lai, Sufen Sofia (1999). "From Cross-Dressing Daughter to Lady Knight Errant: The Origin and Evolution of Chinese Women Warriors," in Sherry J. Mou (ed.), *Presence and Presentation: Women in the Chinese Literati Tradition*. New York: St. Martin's Press.

Laplanche, J. and Pontalis J.B. (1988). *The Language of Psychoanalysis*, trans. Donald Nicholson Smith. London: Karnac Books and the Institute of Psychoanalysis.

Lau, Kwok Wah Jenny and Lee Palmer, Augusta (2003). "Of Executioners and Courtesans: The Performance of Gender in Hong Kong Cinema of the 1990s," in Jenny Kwok Wah Lau (ed.), *Multiple Modernities: Cinemas and Popular Media in Transcultural East Asia*. Philadelphia: Temple University Press.

Lau, Shing Hon (ed.) (1980). *A Study of the Hong Kong Martial Arts Film*. Hong Kong: Hong Kong International Film Festival/Urban Council.

Lee, Kam Wing (1985). The Secret of Seven-Star Mantis Style, trans. Lee Kam Hoi. Hong Kong: Bok Lei Tat Inc.

Leung, Ting (1988). *Shaolin Ten-Animal Form of Kwan Tak Hing*. Hong Kong: Leung Ting Company.

Lévi-Strauss, Claude (1965). "The Structural Study of Myth," in Hazard Adams and Leroy Searle (eds.), *Critical Theory Since 1965*. Tallahassee: University Press of Florida, 605–23.

———— (1969). *The Elementary Structures of Kinship,* trans. J. Harle Bell et al. Boston: Beacon Press.

Logan, Bey (1995). *Hong Kong Action Cinema*. London: Titan.

———— (1999a). *Wong Fei Hung*. Hong Kong: Media Asia.

———— (1999b). "Fong Sai Yuk: Hong Kong's First Action Hero," *Impact*, 95: 30–2.

Mackerras, Colin (1975). *Peking Opera*. Oxford, New York and Hong Kong: Oxford University Press.

Mao, Tse Tung (1967). *On Literature and Art*. Beijing: Foreign Languages Press.

Mulvey Laura (1989a). "Visual Pleasure and Narrative Cinema," in *Visual and Other Pleasures*. Bloomington: Indiana University Press.

———— (1989b). "Afterthoughts on 'Visual Pleasure and Narrative Cinema' inspired by King Vidor's *Duel in the Sun* (1946)," in *Visual and Other Pleasures*.

Pyle, Michael and Linda Miles (1979). *The Movie Brats: How the Film Generation Took over Hollywood*. New York: Holt, Reinhart and Winston.

Ritson, Joseph (ed.) (1997). *Robin Hood: A Collection of All the Ancient Poems, Songs and Ballads, Now Extant Relative to That Celebrated English Outlaw*. London: Routledge/Thoemmes Press.

Schipper, Kristofer. (1993). *The Taoist Body*. Berkley, CA: University of California Press.

Scott A.C. (1983). "The Performance of Classical Theater," in Colin Mackerras (ed.), *Chinese Theatre: From Its Origins to the Present Day*. Honolulu: University of Hawaii Press.

Silverman, Kaja (1996). *The Threshold of the Visible World*. New York, London: Routledge.

Smith, Peter (1995). "Yuen Woo Ping — a Tiger Uncaged," in Rick Baker and Toby Russell (eds.), *The Essential Guide to the Best of Eastern Heroes*. London: Eastern Heroes Publications, 64–7.

Spence, Jonathan D. (1990). *The Search For Modern China*. New York: W. W. Norton & Company.

Stokes, Lisa and Michael Hoover (1999). *City on Fire: Hong Kong Cinema*. London: Verso.

———— (2000). "An Interview with Donnie Yen," *Asian Cult Cinema*, 29: 48–62.

Tasker, Yvonne (1993). *Spectacular Bodies: Gender, Genre and the Action Cinema*. London and New York: Routledge.

Teo, Stephen (1997). *Hong Kong Cinema: The Extra Dimension*. London: BFI.

Tsai, Henry Shih-Shan (1995). *The Eunuchs in the Ming Dynasty*. Albany, NY: State University of New York Press.

Vojković, Sasha (2001). *Subjectivity in the New Hollywood Cinema: Fathers, Sons and Other Ghosts.* Amsterdam: ASCA Press.

———— (2004). "Hong Kong Cinema and the Art of Countering Territorial Regimes: Women Warriors, Wicked Eunuchs and Soccer Players from Shaolin," in Joost de Bloois, Sjef Houppermans, Frans-Willem Korsten (eds.), *Discernments: Deleuzian Aesthetics.* Amsterdam; Kenilworth, NJ: Rodopi.

Waley, Arthur (1994). *The Way and Its Power: A Study of the Tao Te Ching and Its Place in Chinese Thought.* New York: Grove Press.

Williams, Tony (1998). "Kwan Tak Hing and the New Generation," *Asian Cinema* 10, 1: 71–7.

Yang, Jeff (2003). *Once Upon a Time in China: A Guide to Hong Kong, Taiwanese, and Mainland Chinese Cinema.* New York, London, Toronto, Sydney: Atria Books.

Yau, Esther C. M. (ed.) (2001). *At Full Speed: Hong Kong Cinema in a Borderless World.* Minneapolis: University of Minnesota Press.

Zhang Che (Chand Che) (1999). "Creating the Martial Arts Film and the Hong Kong Cinema Style," in *The Making of Martial Arts Films: As Told by Film-makers and Stars.* Hong Kong: Hong Kong Film Archive/Provisional Urban Council, 16–24.